SUSTAINING
A HEALTHY
MINISTERIAL
WORKPLACE

SUSTAINING A HEALTHY MINISTERIAL WORKPLACE

BARBARA SUTTON AND
VICTOR KLIMOSKI

FOREWORD BY KERRY ALYS ROBINSON

Paulist Press
New York / Mahwah, NJ

Scripture texts in this work are taken from the *New American Bible, revised edition* © 2010, 1991, 1986, 1970 Confraternity of Christian Doctrine, Washington, DC, and are used by permission of the copyright owner. All Rights Reserved. No part of the New American Bible may be reproduced in any form without permission in writing from the copyright owner.

C. Vanessa White's talk from the 2020 CTSA that appears in chapter 6 is reproduced here with her permission.

Cover image by jensenartofficial / Pixabay.com
Cover design by Joe Gallagher
Book design by Lynn Else

Copyright © 2024 by Barbara Sutton and Victor Klimoski

All rights reserved. No part of this publication may be reproduced, stored in a retrieval system, or transmitted in any form or by any means, electronic, mechanical, photocopying, recording, scanning, or otherwise, without either the prior written permission of the Publisher, or authorization through payment of the appropriate per-copy fee to the Copyright Clearance Center, Inc., www.copyright.com. Requests to the Publisher for permission should be addressed to the Permissions Department, Paulist Press, permissions@paulistpress.com.

Library of Congress Cataloging-in-Publication Data
Names: Sutton, Barbara Ann, author. | Klimoski, Victor J., author.
Title: Sustaining a healthy ministerial workplace / Barbara Sutton and Victor Klimoski ; foreword by Kerry Alys Robinson.
Description: New York, Mahwah, NJ: Paulist Press, [2024] | Includes bibliographical references and index. | Summary: "This book equips pastoral leaders, ordained and lay, to minister through situations in which there are misunderstandings or conflicts rooted in differences with a broader and deeper understanding of what they can do to create and sustain healthy ministerial workplaces"—Provided by publisher.
Identifiers: LCCN 2024001812 (print) | LCCN 2024001813 (ebook) | ISBN 9780809157082 (paperback) | ISBN 9780809188635 (ebook)
Subjects: LCSH: Church work. | Conflict management—Religious aspects—Christianity.
Classification: LCC BV4400 .S788 2024 (print) | LCC BV4400 (ebook) | DDC 253—dc23/eng/20240708
LC record available at https://lccn.loc.gov/2024001812
LC ebook record available at https://lccn.loc.gov/2024001813

ISBN 978-0-8091-5708-2 (paperback)
ISBN 978-0-8091-8863-5 (e-book)

Published by Paulist Press
997 Macarthur Boulevard
Mahwah, New Jersey 07430
www.paulistpress.com

Printed and bound in the
United States of America

To our co-workers and friends, especially
Virgina Stillwell,
with admiration and deep gratitude

CONTENTS

List of Illustrations ix

List of Tables xi

Foreword xiii
    Kerry Alys Robinson

Preface xvii

Acknowledgements xxiii

Chapter 1: Stories from the Vineyard 1

Chapter 2: From Field Hospital to Thriving Vineyard 23

Chapter 3: Beyond the Single Story 43

Chapter 4: Called to Be Extraordinary 80

Chapter 5: Creating a New Story 102

Chapter 6: The Way Forward 145

Appendices 151
    A. Index for Healthy Ministerial Workplaces 151
    B. Reflection Guide: A Covenant-Based Ministry 158
    C. Learning from Our Stories: Principles for Productive Discussions 166
    D. Using the Narratives and Theological Reflections for Ongoing Formation 173

CONTENTS

Notes 175

Bibliography 187

Index 195

ILLUSTRATIONS

Figure 3.1: Primary Lens of Culture 45

Figure 3.2: Identity Mapping 59

Figure 3.3: Diverse Cultural Values 60

Figure 3.4: Mapping Cultural Identities for Mexico and the United States 68

Figure 3.5: Mapping a Cultural Identity for Traditionalists (1915–1945) 69

Figure 3.6: Mapping a Cultural Identity for Baby Boomers (1946–1964) 69

Figure 3.7: Mapping a Cultural Identity for Gen X (1965–1980) 69

Figure 3.8: Mapping a Cultural Identity for Millennials (1981–1996) 70

Figure 3.9: Mapping a Cultural Identity for Gen Z (1997–2013) 70

Figure 3.10: Mapping Our Strengths 71

Figure 3.11: Mapping across Differences 73

TABLES

Table 2.1: Practices for Community Self-Assessment 34

Table 2.2: Practices for Control Self-Assessment 35

Table 2.3: Practices for Fairness Self-Assessment 36

Table 2.4: Practices for Reward Self-Assessment 37

Table 2.5: Practices for Workload Self-Assessment 37

Table 2.6: Practices for Values Self-Assessment 38

Table 2.7: Practices for Financial Well-Being Self-Assessment............39

Table 2.8: Practices for Vocation Self-Assessment 40

Table 3.1: Mapping Differences within a Team 67

Table 4.1: Sample Item from Reflective Guide...98

FOREWORD

The opportunity to participate in a 2019 symposium titled "Sustaining a Healthy Ministerial Workplace" meant I would get to be in the company of dedicated and experienced ordained and lay ministers, many of whom I knew personally, all of whom I had long admired and respected. Moreover, Barbara Sutton and Victor Klimoski, the hosts of the conference and authors/editors of this book, invited me to deliver a keynote. They asked me to address this critically important question: How can the Church and its leadership influence a healthy workplace and be committed and visible in creating a new story?

I have worked to strengthen the Church all of my adult life and to equip its leaders to be exceptionally good stewards of what has been entrusted to them. I yearn for the Church to draw from the wisdom of its faith and to benefit from the best managerial practices in order to ensure healthy workplace environments. This is what faithful stewardship requires, especially in caring for our most precious asset: people.

The invitation to speak about healthy workplaces encouraged my own personal, vocational, and professional reflection on the topic. How were the Catholic organizations in which I had a leadership role faring? How healthy was our workplace? This introspection took on an even more profound importance when the entire world confronted the consequences of the COVID-19 pandemic in 2020. Overnight for many, the workplace became virtual, and health was a constant, precarious concern. The individual and collective impact of the pandemic required an even greater level of care and responsibility for leaders.

The "Sustaining a Healthy Ministerial Workplace" symposium had to become a series of online sessions over several months. And it was against this backdrop, in this context, in the midst of a pandemic of uncertainty and disruption, that I offered ten maxims designed to help create and foster a healthy culture and environment for work.

1. **People first.** Begin with acknowledging the people with whom you are present, online or in person. Put people first before work tasks, accomplishments, projects, deadlines, procedures, policies, and agendas. Err on the side of compassion and kindness. Pray together. Commit to deep listening and care.

2. **Gratitude.** Express gratitude. Acknowledge the particular dedication, hard work, accomplishments, perseverance, acts of compassion, positive qualities, and strengths members of the pastoral team and staff manifest. Prayer itself can often be an expression of gratitude.

3. **Be positive.** Get in the habit of recalling what it is you most love about being Catholic. The best advice I can offer in times of anguish when the institutional Church fails to live up to its potential or manifests ignoble qualities comes from my teacher and spiritual director, Sister of Mercy Margaret Farley. She said, "Remember what it is you most love about the Church and membership in it. Name what you love. Claim what you love. It will provide ballast to allow you to navigate with fidelity and focus when you are disappointed and discouraged."

4. **Go slow to go far.** Replenish. Be present to the present. Remain truthful and positive. Keep perspective. Think about what needs to be done right now and what needs to be prepared for in the future and help your co-workers discern this.

5. **Cultivate joy.** It can be done, and it can be fun. Both convictions and commitments matter. Notice and acknowledge even small details that bring you and your co-workers joy. Celebrate what is right in order to find the energy to fix what is wrong.

6. **Be solution oriented.** Communicate solutions, not only problems. Communicate with consistency and frequency. Be transparent. Assume nothing. Explaining everything is a good practice to cultivate.

7. **Be generous.** Extend the benefit of the doubt to others. Presume goodness in others, especially your co-workers. We are all called

Foreword

to be generous and to be catalysts to inspire generosity in others. Generosity is humankind's birthright.

8. **Diversity strengthens leadership.** Effective, co-responsible leadership depends on diversity. Diversity matters. We are all myopic by ourselves or within our own narrowly defined groups. We only know what we know. Who is at the tables of decision-making matters.

9. **Emulate what you advocate.** Lead with core values, gospel values. Live out of these core values. Live out of mission in adaptable ways. Be nimble. Practice innovation and creativity. Healthy workplace cultures must be made clear and evidenced by leaders.

10. **Be the reason for someone's hope each day.** Deep within the Catholic imagination is the paschal mystery, the conviction that out of suffering and death comes new life. People of faith are called to be hopeful. We are called to bear witness to new life. Hope is a powerful virtue and grace to extend.

Let these maxims accompany you as you immerse yourself in the powerful stories and pastoral reflections in this volume. Approach it as a retreat in book form and accept its invitation to read and interpret your own experience alongside what the contributors offer. A reflective reading of a book like this becomes a gift because it can help sharpen the guiding vision and values of those committed to pastoral ministry and the gospel it proclaims.

Thank you for investing your time and attention to examine and prioritize habits, practices, and commitments, as leaders and co-workers in faith, to ensure healthy ministerial workplaces.

Kerry Alys Robinson
Woodbridge, Connecticut

PREFACE

We began this book with a well-focused goal: to bring together the information and results of a conference launched in 2020 on creating healthy ministerial workplaces. But as we allowed what we learned from participants to lead us more deeply into the topic, we began to change. Each of us brings to this book long careers in ministry and ministry formation. We have been fortunate to work with scores of lay ecclesial ministers, clergy, and parish staffs on issues arising from the workplace. Those women and men have been teachers to us, challenging our assumptions and expanding our understanding of the complexity that surrounds people working together to advance the gospel. We are indebted as well to conversations, many convened by the Lilly Endowment, where people from seminaries and schools of theology across the country shared what they have learned about ministry and congregational life.

This book is primarily our effort to advance a broader conversation among pastoral leaders about how to ensure that the structures of ministerial practice serve the effectiveness of ministry and enrich the lives of ministers themselves. At the outset, we want to emphasize that while this book has a particular concern for lay ecclesial ministers, it is not written in opposition to clergy or bishops. For that reason, when we use the term *co-workers*, we intend it to include both ordained and lay ecclesial ministers. Healthy workplaces matter for everyone in ministry. As we learned from Barbara's research, more often the issue is not ministerial burnout as much as co-workers finding themselves disengaging, feeling alienated from the very calling that galvanized their life and vocational mission. This book is written as an invitation to readers to come to it with their experiences, concerns, and curiosity. For that reason, we provide opportunities to pause and reflect because we want readers to be active participants in their own processes of discovery, challenging our conclusions and leveraging our recommendations as sources for action.

The pauses for reflection, then, provide space to align one's own experience with concepts we present. These pauses are a way to practice being an inner observer of one's own thoughts and emotions. This interrupts automatic responses (e.g., "That doesn't happen here" or "I can't see how that idea makes a difference or is even possible") and uses present moment integration to manage emotions and minimize unconscious reactivity. Pausing, accompanied by some deep breathing, helps one to recognize an emotional charge in oneself when confronted by something challenging our point of view. Doing so makes it possible to *respond* rather than *react*. When we respond, we bring our best insights into what is being discussed or experienced; when we react, what we do or say most often comes from a place of resistance or defensiveness. The more we can respond as we minister across our differences, the greater the chance we have to build and sustain healthy, inclusive workplace alliances.

Early on we determined that we would avoid as much as possible one more rehearsal of all that seems wrong in the organizational life of Church ministry. This decision strengthened as we journeyed for nearly two years with our material. If we wanted to initiate conversation among all the Church's ministers leading to deep culture change, we needed to position our ideas in a way that encouraged co-workers to claim and live into their power to collaboratively create a new future.

That is one of the reasons a focus on cultural differences emerged halfway in writing the book. Barbara's current position involves her leadership of a project in the Saint Cloud Diocese seeking to transform how co-workers and parishioners alike learn to build community in a rapidly shifting cultural landscape. The insights she was gaining about intercultural and cross-cultural learning offered a new lens for considering the challenges and opportunities in healthy workplaces. While we knew from our extensive work with co-workers that workplace health was not limited to better wages and benefit packages or a well-written employee handbook, we came to see that healthy workplaces depend on co-workers' awareness of the cultural influences that shape how they approach their workplaces and the degree to which they are ready to effect real, sustainable change. We were also led to reappraise how we were integrating the concept of covenant into our views on renewing

Preface

the vineyard of the Lord. It was always part of our thinking even as we planned the original conference in 2020. While we intuitively believed that covenant should be animating the spirit of ministerial workplaces, we did not realize how demanding that would be. To be in covenant is to engage new forms of leadership and co-responsibility for the health of ministry. Chapter 4 details the promise of a covenant-based ministry as well as the deep challenge it presents for co-workers.

THE STRUCTURE OF THE BOOK

The structure of the book seeks to embody what we have learned. Chapter 1 presents eight stories written by people who were actively engaged in Church ministry. Jessie Bazan, a consultant to the project, provides a framework for understanding how the stories emerged over two years as we worked with the ministers to illustrate eight elements of a healthy ministerial workplace. While there is an edge in some of the stories, the purpose of each story is to ensure that the voices of ministers shape what we know about the practice of ministry. These stories find their completion in chapter 5, where the writers offer individual theological and pastoral reflections that flow from the stories they have shared. These reflections are more than a soft landing for the stories. They model how experience teaches, how we come to understand ourselves and our experience by turning to the wisdom of our theological heritage.

We have developed a way for individuals and ministry teams to use the stories and their accompanying theological reflections for ongoing formation. Those guides can be found in the appendices. They seek to encourage co-workers to tend to their own stories of ministry bonded to the theological reflection modeled by our writers. Together, experiences that catch our attention can lead us to appreciate what they reveal about ourselves, give us perspective, and enable us to probe how such experiences reveal the movement of God. It is this movement that can effect the sort of cultural change in the workplace we advocate.

Chapter 2 summarizes research by Barbara on burnout in ministry and what we learned from it. She began with the working assumption that burnout was the most pressing issue in workplace dissatisfaction. In fact, the major dilemma is disengagement. The chapter also introduces the eight elements of a healthy ministerial workplace drawn from the extensive research by Christina Maslach and her associates. They identified six of the elements we address: community, values, fairness, reward, workload, and control. We added two other elements recommended by pastoral consultants: vocation and financial well-being. In addition, we developed an index that co-workers can use to gain insight into how those elements might flourish or languish. We include that index as part of the presentation of the elements in chapter 2.

In chapter 3, we explore the landscape of culture and difference. While many of us in the dominant culture might assume that cultural differences are largely ethnic and racial, it is in actuality much broader. Surely, multicultural differences are real and demand our response in a Church rapidly diversifying. It would be misleading, however, to think that only "they" represent cultural differences. As readers learn in chapter 3, every one of us is formed in several cultures that affect how we see and interpret the world. When we gather around a table to talk about our work, the differences we carry in their many forms are active. Being aware of the composition of our identity, learning the value of cultural humility in the face of wide-ranging diversity, and being consistent in the skills needed to minister across differences for the great mission we share are a steep and unavoidable challenge.

Finding the motivation to engage this challenge led us to a clear sense of the importance a covenant orientation in ministry plays. Chapter 4 lays out our argument. Too often someone suggests that simply having better business practices will improve the conditions for Church ministry. Obviously, that is true at a functional level. Even good businesses, however, are reexamining what needs to happen at a deeper relationship level to engage and nurture committed employees. Covenant used here is the basis and the sustaining motivation for a culture change in which everyone is included, valued, respected, and a contributing member of how we work together. As readers will discover, some of the best insights into a covenant orientation come from the leadership models in other cultures. It isn't that they necessarily directly discuss covenant, but the values and attitudes that govern their ways of leading are very congruent with what a covenant-based ministry requires.

Chapter 5 returns readers to the theological reflections of the stories in chapter 1. As the writers considered their stories against a broader, richer background of theological and pastoral wisdom, their experiences moved them to a new level of insight. If there is a perceptible tension in any of the stories, there is a bright light of hope in each related reflection. This is not a case of putting a happy face on a problem or finding a happy ending. Cultural change is hard work. There is no rest from it or coasting. Everything we do has the potential to teach us—if we spend time going deeper, recalling our foundations, and engaging mindfully with better and more effective skills.

In chapter 6, we provide a summary of the journey taken in the book and identify the makings of a new story. Readers, in conversation with others, are the authors of what will happen next. Our work is predicated on a pastoral leader's ability for self-awareness and to inspire efficacy in others. To achieve this change we believe all pastoral leaders seek, we identify six strategies embedded in the book that can guide and encourage lay ecclesial ministers and clergy as they work toward a new story, a new future. For that work ahead, C. Vanessa White provides a concluding exhortation in the final chapter meant to call co-workers to action: to be bold, to believe in one's agency, and to embrace the mystery and demand of a covenant way of ministering for the sake of the gospel and the transformation of the world.

As we make the necessary shifts in internal awareness, a natural generosity arises within us, and we seek to share our gifts of care and wisdom as a lasting legacy. It is our hope that we inspire and mobilize the Church to engage the learning required to address competently the challenges that we face in co-workers' engagement and our ability to work across differences.

ACKNOWLEDGEMENTS

This book emerged from a project funded by the Association for Theological Schools through its Economic Challenges Facing Future Church Ministers initiative. We were able to continue building on that work through a Thriving Congregations grant from the Lilly Endowment. We are grateful to both organizations for their support.

Sustaining a healthy ministerial workplace depends on many co-workers.

- We benefited immensely from the participation of our writers: Kristi Bivens, Robert Choiniere, Timothy Johnston, Bridgette Klawitter, Dorice Law, Kyle Lechtenberg, Yaret Macedo, and Jim Wahl. They each contributed their pastoral experience and thoughtful theological reflection for the benefit of all who share the ministry they love.
- Jessie Bazan, C. Vanessa White, and Kerry Robinson were part of the original conference. Their ideas enrich the book.
- Cindy Gonzalez gave us editorial guidance to sharpen our intercultural understanding, Joe Towalski provided detailed editing of the manuscript, and Barb Simon-Johnson insured that the graphics used enhanced reader understanding.
- Our concern for ministerial workplaces is shared by other leadership organizations who joined us as partners in exploring ideas at the heart of this book: the Association for Graduate Programs in Ministry, the Diocese of Saint Cloud, the Federation of Pastoral Institutes, and the National Association of Lay Ministers.
- Good ideas blossom in the right setting. We were fortunate to gather as a writing team and with our writers and partners at Saint John's

Abbey Guesthouse. The spirit of hospitality provided a welcoming space for crucial conversations to write and think.

Finally, we express thanks for the counsel and help of Paul McMahon and Donna Crilly at Paulist Press to bring this project to completion.

Chapter 1

STORIES FROM THE VINEYARD

The eight narratives that follow tell stories related to one of the elements of a healthy ministerial workplace. Many of the stories reflect an experience that was disorienting for the writer. Over retellings of the story, each author sharpened her or his point of entry, trying to show how the absence or compromise of an element impacted the ministry and the person of the minister. The reflection questions at the end of each story invite readers to consider it in light of their own experience. The objective in reading the story is not to agree or disagree with it. Rather, we probe any story to discover how it can help us see more clearly the challenges and opportunities we encounter in the practice of ministry and the action needed to stay at the task of creating healthy workplaces. Jessie Bazan, whom we asked to observe the process as these stories were created and refined, offers rich insights on the significance of the process of storytelling. Jessie is a theologian and program associate for the Collegeville Institute for Ecumenical and Cultural Research and is the editor and coauthor of *Dear Joan Chittister: Conversations with Women in the Church* (2019). She regularly contributes to *U.S. Catholic* and writes for both the Liturgical Press and Liturgy Training Publications (LTP).

As important as these stories are, crafted diligently by their authors, they always find completion in the pastoral commentaries presented in chapter 5. In them the writers embraced the challenge to delve into their experience and reflect on the movement of God in them as well as insights from the Church's tradition, Scripture, and the wisdom of others who study these issues. None of the writers suggest they have the answer. They are confident, however, that the process of examining real-life challenges that have impacted them draws them beyond lament to a new sense of agency for change.

INTRODUCTION
Jessie Bazan

> The sacred thing about being human is that no matter how hard we try to get rid of them, our stories are our stories. They are carried inside us; they hover over us; they are the tools we use to explain ourselves to one another, to connect. We cannot take away the experiences of others, but we can learn from them. We can take them and say: What's next to make the world better?[1]
>
> Kaitlin B. Curtice

Stories rose like incense across the cramped conference room. Scribbles adorned the white board walls. Muffins and mixed nuts sat as offerings in the corner. For three days, Saint John's Abbey Guesthouse space served as a sanctuary for storytellers. These storytellers all work as lay ecclesial ministers in the Roman Catholic Church. They hold a variety of positions in parishes, diocesan offices, chaplaincies, Catholic colleges, and seminaries. They hail from across the country. All of them dedicate their lives to Church ministry—and all of them experienced challenges along the way.

What you will read here is the result of significant discernment. Each writer had to consider, "Is it safe to share my story publicly? Am I ready to return to this difficult moment from my past?" The writers also wrestled with the theological implications of their stories. "How does my story reflect the Christian tradition? What might my story be calling the Church to do today?"

"This is the hardest writing I've done," lamented one author as he slumped into his seat at the end of a session. Seven heads nodded in agreement. Empathy is perhaps the greatest gift the writers give one another. Another chimed in: "I'm very nervous to share this story, but I'm sharing it to better the workplace for others."

These lay ministers offer their stories to make the Church a healthier, more just place to work. The clerical abuse and cover-up crisis certainly heightened issues between clergy and laity in the ministerial workplace. The crisis left many lay ministers with an awful choice: speak up and get fired, or remain silent and allow the abuse to continue. Resulting lawsuits left some parishes with little money to pay lay ministers. Some employees were laid off while others continued the same work as "volunteers." Lay ministers worldwide felt the impact of the hierarchy's collective failure to be transparent and accountable. The fallout is far from over.

Still, divisions in the ministerial workplace run deeper. This book explores eight issues common to ministerial workplaces: vocation, community, values, control, reward, workload, fairness, and financial well-being. Each writer shares real stories that illuminates one of the issues. In this way, the book is a theological reflection on the ministerial workplace that starts with experience as the first "text." It cannot be said enough: sharing these stories was no easy task.

Nevertheless, the writers persisted. They persisted because they—we—are covenant people. We believe in a God who keeps promises, who formed our ancestors and who forms us to do the same. In the waters of baptism, we each entered into a covenant with Jesus Christ, his death, and resurrection. The baptismal covenant stems from the old covenant made throughout salvation history, from the very beginning of creation to Noah's time on the ark, to the Israelites crossing the Red Sea, and more. Repeatedly, God shows faithfulness to God's beloved people by affirming their covenantal relationship.

The concept of covenant grounds the work of this book as lay ministers explore how to strengthen relationships within the ministerial workplace. We are convinced that ministerial workplaces can thrive when co-workers honor the callings of one another. The covenant between God and David as told in 2 Samuel 6:17–19 was especially formative for this book. The writers spent time with this Scripture passage and corresponding illumination from *The Saint John's Bible* in a process called *visio divina*—a prayer practice that uses both text and art to help individuals encounter the living word of God.

A few insights from our prayer time help to set the context for reading these stories:

- **Showing up involves sacrifice.** The people who traveled to see the ark of the Lord did so in the midst of everyday life. Who did they leave behind? What other responsibilities did they set aside? Lay ministers ask similar questions today. Many of us work long hours, during the evenings and on weekends. We sacrifice our family life. We know we do not get paid nearly as much as we would if we took our gifts to a secular organization. We sacrifice financial security. A covenant of lay ministry is a covenant of sacrifice.

- **Endings and beginnings can both be holy.** With the tent in place, David "sacrificed burnt offerings and communion offerings before the Lord." We played around with the juxtaposition of "burnt" and "communion." The former conjures images of decay and ending, while the latter points to coming together and beginning new life. Both matter for the health of covenant relationships. What injustices need to burn in ministerial workplaces? Where should we fan the flames of communion?

- **God's blessings are for everyone.** David distributed the Lord's blessings "among all the people, the entire multitude of Israel, to every man and woman." The gifts lay ministers bring to the ministerial workplace vary greatly. God blesses each with particular strengths for the building up of the kingdom. What would it look like if communities lifted up and affirmed the gifts of all their ministers?

- **The ark and the people move.** David pitched a tent for the ark of the Lord. He did not build a cement structure. Our God cannot be boxed in. Neither should lay ministers. What worked fifty or even five years ago may not serve today's Church in the same way. The ministerial workplace is dynamic. It needs to expand with the needs of the world.

- **The work of the people continues.** Freshly blessed, "all the people returned to their homes." What did the encounter with God awaken in them? How were they transformed? God also sends lay ministers today into the world, beyond the Church walls, to share the good news. With God as our strength and guide, we live as covenant people in our homes, workplaces, community centers, and streets.

May the stories and insights of these heartfelt stories and the reflections they called forth from their authors deepen a sense of the power of covenant and inspire greater justice and health in the ministerial workplace.

Stories from the Vineyard

VOCATION: CALLED AT THIS TIME, TO THIS WORK

Kristi Bivens

Kristi Bivens is the associate director of lay leadership formation for the Diocese of St. Cloud. She spent ten years previously as a lay ecclesial minister in two parishes in western rural Minnesota. In addition to her master of divinity degree from Saint John's School of Theology and Seminary, she is completing a graduate certificate in leading contemplative groups and retreats.

"What is vocation?" We were reflecting on the question in small groups at a staff retreat. At the table were Catholics and non-Catholics, those with ministry and theological formation and those without. One person offered the standard Church reply, "Priesthood, religious life, marriage, and the single life." Nods around the table. "We need more priests and religious." More nods. Except for one co-worker who said without a hint of doubt, "I don't believe that the single life is a vocation."

As a single, Catholic woman who has been in Church ministry her entire adult life, conversations about vocation usually leave me angry. My understanding of vocation, influenced by my mentors and my theological education, has outgrown the tiresome clichés. Normally, I would let my co-worker's comment play itself out, but he proceeded to explain the single life was not a vocation because it is never mentioned in official Church documents. I stopped listening because my inner monologue was going crazy. "No single life? And we never talk about lay ministry as a vocation? I don't have a place in this Church, once again!" I could not stay silent this time.

"So, what you are telling me," I began, "is that I have no vocation. I am single, which you say is not a vocation. I have committed my life to Church ministry, which you say is not a vocation." A priest sitting next to me chimed in, "The single life is a vocation." The young man who had claimed the opposite said nothing. Someone else in the group moved the conversation to the next question. No one was willing to engage the impasse. I left that meeting angry and hurt that vocation for too many people hinges on my getting married or entering a convent. I wondered why I bothered staying with something that seemed to carry so little meaning for some people.

But my sense of vocation is deeper than unreflective comments about what vocation is. My current job in ministry as associate director of lay leadership formation is relatively new and part of a new diocesan initiative, Emmaus Institute for Ministry Formation. It exists to form laypeople for ministry and Latino men for the permanent diaconate. Getting the program off the ground in just four short months was challenging but worth every bit of stress. I loved the work. In the first weekend of classes, the spirit of celebration and excitement was palpable. We had sixty people from all levels of society, speaking two different languages, who were on fire to learn more about their faith and their ministry. The Church *was* on fire!

I couldn't sleep that night and couldn't wait to get back to work to tell everyone about it. Some were just as excited as I was, some were politely affirming, and others had no reaction. As the month went on, I lost some of my original energy and enthusiasm and thought that when the Institute gathered again in October, participants would be past the novelty. I was dead wrong. Every weekend has been filled with energy and excitement, giving me hope for the Church. The people coming want to serve in the name of Jesus and do it well. These are people who recognize the reality of vocation unbound from ordination and vows.

After a year in this position, I always respond to questions about how I like my work with the same statement: "I love what I am doing." The answer and the experience from which it comes help me manage my annoyance when people try to dismiss or trivialize my calling. I can say with great confidence, "God has called me into this time and place to do the work that I am doing. Everything I have done has led me here. This is my ministry. This is my vocation."

Frederick Buechner once defined vocation as "the place where your deep gladness meets the world's deep need." My deep gladness is providing formation and education to help people grow in their call to service in the Church. The world's deep need is well-formed lay ministers who help continue and extend the mission of Jesus Christ. We do not do this apart from the ordained but alongside them. I believe God has called me in this moment to move the conversation to a new level.

Questions about whether I "really" have a vocation might fray my nerves a bit, but they no longer throw me off track. I continue to tell my story about vocation. I continue to discern my vocation and listen for the ways in which the Holy Spirit is calling me. I take advantage of ways to broaden discussion of vocation. Most importantly, my formation, theological education, and ministerial experience confirm that lay ecclesial ministry *is* a vocation done in the name of the Church. It is there that my deep gladness and the world's deep need joyously meet.

PAUSE FOR REFLECTION
- With whom or what do you identify in this narrative?
- What biases are evident?
- How are power differences present?
- How would you respond differently?

COMMUNITY: CREATING SPACE FOR GOSPEL VALUES TO THRIVE

Dorice Law

Dorice Law earned her master of divinity degree at Saint John's School of Theology and Seminary. During that time, she served with campus ministry as director of social justice and director of religious formation. After completing four units of CPE at Park Nicollet Methodist Hospital, she served as chaplain at Friendship Village, was a pastoral associate at Ascension Catholic Church, 2016–2018, and served as chaplain at Catholic Eldercare, 2019–2021.

Despite low pay and part-time hours, it looked like a dream first job after completing my master of divinity degree and yearlong clinical pastoral education (CPE) residency. I was now a chaplain for the skilled nursing and memory care units at an upscale senior community. My immediate supervisor, Morgan, was an ordained minister who worked primarily with the independent-living side of the campus. As a mentor, she brought years of experience and insight.

The only problem was Morgan did not always want to share the stage. In public, she needed me to recognize her as head chaplain, which made sense given her seniority. What I didn't realize was how important it was for me to be liked and accepted and how damaged I would become under Morgan's supervision. Generally, I fit in well. People are often drawn to my genuine affection, concern, and nonjudgmental acceptance. In many ways, however, my presence bothered Morgan. She refused to update our department picture if it meant taking a picture with me, commenting on my high cheekbones as her rationale. Consequently, individual pictures were taken and displayed separately in our designated area of care.

After my first time preaching in the main chapel to our independent-living residents, there was a significant shift in Morgan's behavior toward me. She had offered to attend the service to introduce me and provide support, warning me it was a tough crowd that included accomplished professionals and a few retired ministers. I came well prepared. Using the Scripture of the day from the lectionary, I illustrated the Scripture with a story about a young boy who loses his mother and finds family in his teacher. Residents were very complimentary. The next day Morgan called me into her office. I thought she was going to congratulate me; instead, she critiqued the program's handout. She highlighted inconsistencies in formatting, my poor song selections, and my carelessness in not disclosing to the audience that the story was most likely fictional. She had researched the story's source and found one version stating the story was possibly a fable. She warned me she had to report the incident to our department head, Mrs. Korth. This level of encounter between the two of us would become a regular pattern.

For any number of events, including the Christmas program, I was left out of the planning. With the lack of departmental collaboration, I often felt less like a colleague and more like "the help." Morgan was constantly pushing for me to take some of her workload, even though with my contract of twenty-four hours per week, I was providing spiritual care on three floors for skilled nursing and memory care and programing. To keep the peace, I took over tasks we once shared. Because overtime was not allowed, I often punched off the clock and went back to work. Unfortunately, my successful completion of tasks only seemed to validate Morgan's belief that I could be doing more.

Morgan introduced a workday assessment tool that required me to document the tasks I performed every fifteen minutes. She scheduled my breaks and lunch, doing random check-ups on my progress by email. Her comments tended to be demeaning and demanding. After I showed our department head the evidence of this unjust monitoring, Morgan was immediately released from her supervisory role. Mrs.

Korth appointed herself as my supervisor; unfortunately, my work environment did not improve. For several months, Morgan refused to speak to me, making departmental events unbearable and driving me further into isolation. Sometimes, even Mrs. Korth would ask me to justify my actions, and I suspected Morgan of stirring up mistrust. Every such encounter left me feeling as if my integrity was in question.

The end came surprisingly fast. I was scheduled to work on the Fourth of July. Halfway through my shift, I was notified there were two actively dying residents, one of whom had their grieving family present. I put aside my own family plans and stayed, spending several hours offering prayer and comfort. Soon after, Mrs. Korth called me into her office and demanded an explanation for exceeding my regular hours. The tone of the reprimand echoed the relationship I had had with Morgan. I calmly explained the situation as best as I could and then went to my office to write my two-week notice. There was no place for me there.

PAUSE FOR REFLECTION
- With whom or what do you identify in this narrative?
- What biases are evident?
- How are power differences present?
- How would you respond differently?

VALUES: A SHARED FAITH, A COMMON MISSION

Robert Choiniere

Robert Choiniere is a professor of theology at Fordham University in New York City and currently on sabbatical at the Pontifical Gregorian University in Rome, where he is studying synodality and working with Discerning Leaders, a Jesuit ministry that provides synodal leadership training to Church leaders. He has an extensive background in pastoral planning and ecclesial consultation for several dioceses and chaired the Conference of Pastoral Planning and Council Development (CPPCD). He holds a doctor of ministry from

Fordham University and a master's degree in pastoral ministry from Boston College.

What I remember most from my interview for the new diocesan position of associate director of pastoral planning was the focus on values, priorities, and aspirations. The interview team discussed its vision of the new office, hopes for meaningful collaboration between clergy and laity, and diocesan-wide discernment on mission. Team members also shared concerns about how restructuring might impact the values of community, charity, and hospitality as parishes battled over territory and survival. I accepted the job, feeling called into a challenging environment ripe for renewal through collaboration.

Over the next nine years, I helped guide pastors and lay leaders in processes of consultation, shared decision-making, collaboration, and restructuring. When a financial crunch hit, a permanent deacon who had been a corporate consultant emerged to assist in a large-scale downsizing of the diocesan staff. In his new role, he operated apart from the values of collaboration, consultation, and shared leadership that aligned diocesan ministry as I experienced it. His values seemed to favor efficiency, top-down authority, and less transparency. He eventually became director of both human resources and information technology and shortly thereafter began to deplete the resources of my office. He transferred members of my team just as large projects were due. He limited access to our own data systems, challenged our methodologies, and demanded to personally review our already peer-reviewed procedures. I lost my office, my staff, and was given a desk in a hallway to run the entire reconfiguration effort.

Eventually, my direct boss, the vicar general, was transferred. As I helped him pack up his office for the move, I found a letter from the deacon in which he lambasted all of my initiatives, questioned my professionalism, and called for my termination. When I brought this letter to the vicar general's attention, he dramatically tore it in half and tossed it in the trash. Looking me straight in the eye, he said, "Robert, never do anything if it is not for the glory of God. This letter is all about the glory of man."

A month later, a new vicar general was appointed. I was soon called into a meeting and informed that I was being terminated immediately and the Office of Pastoral Planning was being closed. I was not given a reason. Ten days later I met with the bishop and asked the reason.

Without emotion he said he had no money left to pay me, which was not true. A decade of my life was poured into this ministry that had succeeded even under the most difficult of circumstances. It was what I was called to do. What had happened? Clearly a new culture and mindset were at work but not communicated. Trust eroded, secrecy prevailed, and employee engagement diminished.

It seemed that the top leadership had betrayed their own deepest values.

Four years later, a member of the bishop's curia invited me to a private meeting. He started the conversation strangely, saying, "What I am about to tell you has caused me many sleepless nights and has been a great moral quandary, but you should know why the bishop closed your office and terminated you." He went on to say that at a meeting of the bishop's council, the deacon had presented information to make a case that I was not fit for leadership. I was not to be asked about this evidence, the deacon argued, as I might file a lawsuit for a settlement greater than what my severance would cost the institution. Everyone present was sworn to secrecy. The bishop was convinced, and my termination was sealed with no due process or reason given.

PAUSE FOR REFLECTION
- With whom or what do you identify in this narrative?
- What biases are evident?
- How are power differences present?
- How would you respond differently?

CONTROL: KNOWING WHEN EVERYTHING IS NOT A PRIORITY

Bridget Klawitter

After over thirty years in healthcare, Bridget Klawitter transitioned to parish ministry. She holds a master's degree in administrative leadership and supervision, a master's in ministry (Cardinal Stritch University) and a PhD in urban education (University of Wisconsin–Milwaukee). She has worked in parishes in the Archdiocese of Milwaukee for over fifteen years, serving on various commissions. Bridget is currently the pastoral associate at St. Leonard Catholic Parish and School in Muskegon, Wisconsin, and was certified as a pastoral associate by the Alliance for the Certification of Lay Ecclesial Ministry through the National Association of Lay Ministry (NALM) in 2017. She is an active member of NALM.

It was Monday, my first day in a new position. I had met briefly with my predecessor a few weeks earlier, but that visit was all a blur except for a few scribbled notes. The parish business manager had me fill out necessary "first day" paperwork but did not have time to do more than guide me to my desk. The pastor and several other staff people were off for the day, so I was on my own. The job description I received was pretty general. My desk was empty except for a few hanging file folders, some old purchase orders, and old bulletin inserts. The bookshelves were jam packed with books and magazines—a few familiar, a lot quite dated. On the desk next to the computer was a handwritten list of what was scheduled for me that week. There is nothing like starting with your feet on fire! Thankfully, I had been told that Mondays were the quietest day in the parish for my position. Trying to get my bearings, I prayed that held true.

Where to start? The pastor mentioned in the interview how pleased he was with my background in parish administrative and pastoral duties and was confident I would know what had to be done. "You'll figure it out," he said. But would I? The list by the computer looked so daunting! There were two evening meetings, one involving a moms' ministry and the other the monthly human concerns commission. I was the designated staff liaison for both groups but had no other information other than the date and time of the meetings. There was a baptism preparation class scheduled for another evening with three registered families. The parish had both a traditional and a family program for Christian formation as well as ongoing adult formation offerings. A staff planning meeting on Thursday over lunch would decide on the formation fall programming schedule and topics. Two people had left messages asking for a call back. One was a baptized Catholic seeking confirmation and the other an unbaptized young man desiring to receive sacraments. My head was already spinning on how I would get it all accomplished this first week—or at this pace, given the fact that I was hired for twenty-four hours per week. While my predecessor was contracted for thirty to thirty-two hours per week, the position had been scaled back in the latest budgeting process. Scaled back in time, not responsibilities.

I realized, in that moment, my need to prioritize tasks and organize my attitude and efforts. Prioritizing would allow me to identify the most pressing tasks, so I could focus my energies. Having a positive attitude about what I could realistically accomplish and creating a plan of attack would help me identify questions requiring answers or direction, needed resources, and people to contact. It was a strategy for surviving this first week, but I also had to remind myself that I was well equipped to tackle the challenge. My previous work with adult sacrament preparation and adult formational programs gave me a solid foundation upon which to build. I would need to determine what materials had been used in the past for sacrament preparation and what topics had been covered in the various family and adult formation programs. Armed with that information, I would be able to add my own distinct approaches in collaboration with the pastor.

During the rest of that first week, I was purposeful in spending more time with my ministry colleagues to learn from them about the culture of the parish and the approaches used by my predecessor. The staff seemed to enjoy a fair degree of autonomy in their positions and demonstrated a sincere willingness to share their expertise and suggestions. Although I sensed a bit of possible conflict with one person, it was something I could manage positively. As with each prior position in parish work and in my years in healthcare administration, each colleague was a unique individual with a palette of gifts and talents. Time would help me to determine how I fit in best moving forward, working with them side by side. My experience gave me the capacity to exercise control in "figuring it out." I couldn't help but wonder, however, what would have happened if I had been new to ministry or lacked the background I brought? Is the assumption about "figuring it out" a compliment or an impediment?

PAUSE FOR REFLECTION
- With whom or what do you identify in this narrative?
- What biases are evident?

- How are power differences present?
- How would you respond differently?

REWARD: RECOGNIZING THE DIGNITY OF WHAT WE DO

Kyle Lechtenberg

Kyle Lechtenberg has served in liturgical and music ministries in parish, diocesan, and campus settings and has taught public school vocal music. He holds degrees in music education (University of Northern Iowa) and liturgical studies (University of Notre Dame). He is the author of numerous pastorally focused articles for liturgical and music ministers and has served on the board of the Federation of Diocesan Liturgical Commissions. Kyle is currently a stay-at-home parent while also working with City Voices, a nonprofit organization whose mission is to improve financially disadvantaged students' access to individual music instruction.

As director of music and liturgy preparing Christmas liturgies, I needed to discuss with Jordan, the supervisor of the parish administrative staff, my need for some additional assistance in December. Our office would close for the few days before Christmas, and that meant I would be on my own unless I thought ahead. I had a few small tasks in mind that Reece, our parish secretary and program assistant, could do for me to finalize preparations. This was the usual way we dealt with workflow issues that arose. What promised to be a simple conversation went another way:

"Christmas is coming! I see Reece is going to be gone a couple of days before Christmas and I was wondering if I can talk with him about assisting on a few projects with me."

"He's pretty busy right now and then he's going to be gone the few days before Christmas," Jordan said. "No one is going to be here then, actually. You'll be on your own if you wait until then."

"Yeah, that's why I'm asking now. I thought that maybe I could get ahead of it a little bit and see about help in advance."

"Well, I don't know. Like I said, he's pretty busy. You'll probably be on your own those days. Anyway, Kyle, what could you possibly need assistance with?"

That last comment took me by surprise. We have five Masses, two of which are celebrated simultaneously in separate locations with different musicians, ministers, and so on, and we had arrangements to make for the weekend and holy day that fall while everyone else is off on holiday. We will have three thousand people attending services in a span of eighteen hours. There are worship aids to be printed, music to be collated, ritual texts to be developed and distributed, volunteers to be invited and coordinated. Was Jordan really asking me what I could possibly need assistance with? But I didn't say any of that. I took this statement as an undervaluation of music and liturgy and of me personally. What I did say was, "Oh, you're right. I'll take care of it."

This wasn't the first time something like this happened. Music and liturgy were only a couple of years old as a "department." Previous staffing was part-time and evidently didn't ask much of anyone else on staff. So perhaps requests for support were new, and staff maybe was slow to adjust. I was newly married with an infant daughter at home. Work, even ministry, had a different place in my life after these two changes. Everything was being reordered and prioritized.

All that ran in the background when my colleague said, "What could you possibly need assistance with?" Well, these major liturgies can be beautiful and uplifting for those who attend and can help them to maintain a healthy work-life balance. It is lonely and stressful doing this worthwhile work alone. This work is important, and I want to share it with others. I needed help working on our celebrations for the birth of Jesus!

The simple exchange with Jordan reminded me that ten years of dysfunctional work experiences had reinforced my pattern of being silent and leaving when things got to be too much. In one setting, my pastor favored me to the exclusion of other staff, and in another, my supervisor didn't trust me very much at all and left me alienated from other staff. There was so much potential and possibility in this new setting, and I wanted to discern how to advance in my area of ministry while taking my place at the table. Intangible rewards draw many of us to ministry; I am no exception. I want to know that music and liturgy are important in parish life, that I am valued, and that my unique gifts are valued with no strings attached, other than the tether that binds me to the One who created me.

PAUSE FOR REFLECTION
- With whom or what do you identify in this narrative?
- What biases are evident?
- How are power differences present?
- How would you respond differently?

WORKLOAD: THE CHALLENGE OF BALANCE

Yaret Macedo

Yaret Macedo is the director of administration and pastoral ministries at Immaculate Heart of Mary Parish. She holds a degree in business administration from California State University, Fullerton, and a master's degree in pastoral theology from Loyola Marymount University. Yaret works with the leadership of twenty different ministries, including faith formation programs with the Hispanic and Vietnamese communities. In addition, she oversees all the administrative functions of the parish. Previously, she served for nine years as office manager of the Institute for Pastoral Ministry (IPM) in the Diocese of Orange.

In the summer of 2015, right after graduate school, I began my dream position at my home parish—the newly created position of director of administration and pastoral ministries. On the first weekend, I was officially introduced to the entire community at all nine Masses in a Rite of Commissioning. This was significant for me and our community because I am the first Hispanic lay ecclesial minister in such a position in the Diocese of Orange. It felt like the springtime of ministry as my ministerial identity was being nurtured in the parish.

This is a vibrant community with twenty-five different parish ministries and groups. Our staff consists of four priests, two deacons, four full-time employees, and thirteen part-time employees working in the reception, bookkeeping, faith formation, evangelization, and maintenance departments. In addition, we have about sixty unpaid volunteer ministry leaders from different parish groups and ministries who oversee the thousand-plus parish volunteers. Each weekend, seven thousand parishioners attend one of nine Masses offered in Spanish, Vietnamese, or English.

In my first years, I was responsible for two core ministerial needs: pastoral ministry and organizational development. Each pastoral ministry group required help with organization, collaboration, and guidance. I began coordinating group meetings, organizing parish events with every ministry participating, and working with ministerial workplans to help them gain a sense of direction. Constant restructuring of the administration and organization of the parish has impacted the physical plant itself and resulted in personnel changes. In the midst of this, a new pastor arrived for whom this was his first assignment. To be honest, nothing in my life prepared me for the immensity of the pastoral tasks ahead.

In my third year, two surprise resignations due to health and personal issues caused me to look more closely at the work culture of our parish staff. The first person was the faith formation director, who oversaw the sacramental preparation programs serving 1,500 children and 100 catechists. The second person was a part-time bookkeeper who was not fully knowledgeable in her work area, which only increased her feeling of being overwhelmed. Both said their resignations were due to lack of support from management and insufficient human and financial resources to do their work well. They also felt that needed change was not on the horizon. In the meantime, several other employees requested leaves of absence or took recurring sick days because of exhaustion and discouragement from their daily work. Was our work environment demanding too much from our pastoral staff? Was it driving them to the edge of burnout and disengagement? Why did I not recognize this earlier?

I have discovered that such a large parish with high demands for service for so many people also demands greater care for the personal health of those who serve in these positions. The mix of emotions, the challenges within different ministries, and constant change in the parish structure and staff have been an extraordinary learning experience. After four and half years in my position, I can say that I enjoy being part of this wonderful ministry. At the same time, while I feel the need to be a calming presence for the pastoral team, I have also felt discouraged, disillusioned, and defeated in my ministry. This can leave me feeling emotionally drained at the end of my workday, pulled in different directions, and wanting to escape from all the demands and even the ministry itself. Of greater concern are the instances in which I have put my ministry first before my personal life, believing I was the only one who could get the job done. Consequently, I have depersonalized my co-workers, volunteers, and parishioners on occasion, seeing them as one more problem to be solved. This was deeply distressing because I am a relational person in how I minister. Since day one, I have been available for people to talk, to request, to demand, to feel supported, and to be guided. Proportionately, 60 percent of my time is spent attending to the needs of parishioners and staff while the other 40 percent is given to the administration and organization of the parish.

In a parish like ours that values being vibrant and where the demand for services escalates daily, trying to manage the workload is not easy. No one is exempt from the risks of feeling overwhelmed or of burnout. Staying alert to early warning signs, seeking support and perspectives from others, and working together to achieve balance are indispensable for sustaining a workplace where everyone thrives—even the director of administration and pastoral ministry!

PAUSE FOR REFLECTION
- With whom or what do you identify in this narrative?
- What biases are evident?
- How are power differences present?
- How would you respond differently?

FAIRNESS: PRACTICING JUSTICE, SHOWING CARE

Timothy Johnston

Timothy Johnston serves as a pastoral associate at St. Thomas the Apostle in Chicago's Hyde Park. He holds a master of arts degree in liturgical studies from Saint John's School of Theology and Seminary and in Christian doctrine from Marquette University. Previous to his current position, Timothy served as director of the offices of worship for the Archdiocese of Washington, DC, the Diocese of Salt Lake City, and the Diocese of St. Cloud. He was also an editor and liturgical training consultant for Liturgy Training Publications in the Archdiocese of Chicago. He has published and presented workshops on liturgical formation.

In one of my first ministry positions, I worked with a team of volunteers to prepare a national event for various liturgical ministers. The event was highly successful, grossing ninety thousand dollars—more than we could have imagined. Even better, my department was to receive half. It would be a crucial asset for implementing the strategic plan for ongoing liturgical formation and help the department fulfill its mission to enrich the liturgical life of the community.

In the weeks following the event, I learned that the area supervisor, without consultation, decided to divide the money inequitably between several offices. I was outraged! We had a contract with the sponsoring organization that explicitly stated that any profit would be divided equally between it and the office responsible for liturgical formation. This decision violated the contract. I was disheartened and angry. How could the supervisor be so arbitrary, making a decision that was fundamentally unfair? The lack of transparency and the absence of collegial discernment reinforced a sense I worked in a culture of favoritism and distrust. I felt powerless and unheard. My anger began to affect my health, my relationship with my co-workers, and even my spiritual life. I let my interpretation of the decision fester.

After several weeks passed, I learned that one of my colleagues had approached our supervisor several months before the event and complained that his office and programming would be affected by our event and, therefore, deserved compensation for his office's financial losses. This outraged me and led me to focus on all the negative things I could conjure up about this co-worker: he came late to work, missed scheduled meetings without apology, and disregarded deadlines that affected the work of other offices. He often refused to collaborate, saying, "We tried that before, and it didn't work. Let's stick to what we've always done."

Because his behaviors contradicted the policies in our handbook, I felt strongly that it was unfair that he could "get away" with what I labeled as a scheme. Going behind my back to address our supervisor about the funds was deceitful. I felt like he duped everyone into believing he worked harder, produced more results, and deserved reward for projects, like this event, in which he took no part. His tenure with this organization exceeded mine by twelve years so the supervisor's decision appeared like favoritism and a way to avoid conflict.

After feeling embittered for several months, I gathered the courage to confront my co-worker about what had taken place. This encounter was hostile at best. I aggressively accused him of nurturing and sustaining his position as a beloved or *favored* employee. He was unwilling to acknowledge what I had experienced and felt the decision was just. No reconciliation or resolution was achieved in this meeting.

Next, I scheduled a meeting with our management team to discuss the process used to make this decision. I shared how unfair I felt it was to divvy up the money between the offices without talking with me. As their colleague, I expected them to treat me with respect and as someone who cares about the overall mission. From outside the "favorites" circle, it looked like my co-worker only received the money because of his grumblings so many months earlier. Following several conversations, the management team agreed to review its decision-making process and formulate a more transparent and collegial process—not simply because I complained but because, in the end, it advanced a commitment to fairness for the organization.

PAUSE FOR REFLECTION
- With whom or what do you identify in this narrative?
- What biases are evident?
- How are power differences present?
- How would you respond differently?

FINANCIAL WELL-BEING: THE COSTS OF VOCATIONAL CALL

James Wahl

James Wahl has served as director of music at parishes in California, Arizona, and North Carolina. Since 2010 he has been the director of liturgy and music at St. Francis of Assisi in Raleigh, a parish of over 3,500 families. He holds a bachelor of music degree from California State University, a master's in liturgical music from Saint John's School of Theology and Seminary, and is currently pursuing doctoral studies at the University of Durham, UK, with research on the experience of children at liturgy. He has published and presents nationally on liturgical and catechetical music for children and adults.

Making the decision to travel to India was easy, finding a way to pay for it was the hard part. Our son had moved to a monastery in Bengaluru (Bangalore), India, three months earlier, having been invited to live there with full room and board at no cost. However, worsening conditions associated with his bipolar diagnosis had raised such concerns about his safety that the U.S. State Department had asked us to travel there to help bring him back to the United States for hospitalization. It was a week before Christmas, and we had less than one hundred dollars in our bank accounts and no credit available to us.

Having worked full-time as a pastoral musician for the past twenty years, we had grown accustomed to living paycheck to paycheck. Raising four children on a single salary, the costs of health insurance for my family's chronic medical issues, and high housing costs in areas that could support a full-time musician's salary became a constant classic and admittedly ironic game of robbing Peter to pay Paul. However, this was different. Our son's life was in jeopardy, and we had to make it work. A friend from the parish who had been walking this journey with us for the past several years offered her credit card with no hesitation. We accepted her help, and three days before Christmas 2016, I returned from a whirlwind trip to India with our son, getting him as far as JFK airport, where he had another manic episode. He would spend the next several months between hospitals, jails, and psych wards in New York City, while we managed the emotional and financial stresses of how to care and advocate for him five hundred miles away in Raleigh.

Following the start of the new year, we decided to go public with our struggles, both about our son and our financial situation. We quickly organized an online fundraising campaign to cover the costs of the India trip as well as ongoing and future costs of caring for our son. Within a few days we raised over ten thousand dollars from families and friends, many of them parishioners. The parish community itself rallied around us with prayer, financial support, and meals. However, at the same time, I was facing increased scrutiny from the pastor about my job. In conducting a mid-year review of budgets, he had discovered that the music budget was over by around three thousand dollars. I was, in fact, aware of this, but knew it was due to an error in payroll processing and simply delayed correcting the issue. Instead of asking about the overage, he suddenly became hyperfocused about how the ministry was structured, requiring a change in my responsibilities, an immediate time study of my hours on a thirty-minute basis, and the suspension of stipends for additional musicians.

I was astounded by the timing of these actions and the emotional disconnection with what I was facing on a personal level. Intense budget scrutiny overshadowed any sense of pastoral concern. I was employed by a church known for exemplary pastoral care, yet I had to turn to the healthcare system for that support. My anxiety reached such a high level that doctors were encouraging me to take a leave of absence. While the parish community rallied around me and showed concern for my son, most members were unaware of the professional issues I was now facing. Trust had eroded, and over the next few weeks, the pastor and I met and worked through details with a third party present. Deep inside, I felt shame about our family finances (even though, I am one of the 47 percent of Americans who could not cover a four-hundred-dollar emergency expense), and I was embarrassed at my not attending to the three-thousand-dollar budget correction. The whole situation felt ungodly.

Ultimately, there were no structural changes to the music ministry or my job expectations. However, I acutely felt a lack of equity. I did not have access to the financial security or institutionalized care my pastor could assume for himself. I recognized, as I never fully did before our family crisis, that the system has different standards for what financial well-being means for its ordained and lay ecclesial ministers. This crisis has passed, but what if there is a next time? Is my only choice to take on more outside jobs or leave ministry altogether?

PAUSE FOR REFLECTION
- With whom or what do you identify in this narrative?
- What biases are evident?
- How are power differences present?
- How would you respond differently?

Chapter 2

FROM FIELD HOSPITAL TO THRIVING VINEYARD

The vision for creating and sustaining healthy ministerial workplaces builds on two decades of research as well as working with and listening to lay ecclesial ministers. Three scenarios help to frame what we learned.

First, when studying economic challenges facing Church ministers with a diocesan ecclesial ministry advisory committee, we observed competent lay ecclesial ministers seemingly trapped in a web of tired truth-telling and false consensus. At first, we assumed their vocational aspirations had been smothered as a consequence of burnout. Many experienced the demoralizing impact of the sexual abuse crisis that continues to reverberate. They watch as colleagues in ministry lose their jobs or they themselves feel the tenuousness of their positions as financial support for the Church wanes. They often live in dread as a pastor moves to a new assignment and they wait for his replacement with some trepidation. Moreover, their efforts to advance the mission of the gospel too often are regarded by clergy and parishioners as "nice but not essential." While these realities challenge ecclesial ministers, we have discovered that they are not determining factors in the sense of their core vocational identity.

The second scenario comes from a weekend winetasting at a local vineyard. While there, we saw the sign for a nearby resort welcoming the annual diocesan clergy conference. It caused us to wonder the degree to which clergy ponder the health and vibrancy of the "vineyard of the Lord." We started thinking about an intersection where all the Church's ministers meet, a place for wholehearted conversation on sustaining a healthy ministerial workplace. Each of us has been at this intersection of the known and the unknown about our future as pastoral leaders. At this intersection we are not imagining a negotiating session about the conditions of employment with a little give and take but rather a *repatterning* so that what emerges becomes purposeful and courageous. This was an "aha" moment that more was afloat in our stories than sour grapes between the ordained and those they supervise. We needed to build a bridge, and it would take a good dose of relational humility between the clergy and lay ecclesial ministers to release the potential to thrive and overcome the sense of interpersonal distance.

The third scenario comes from a faculty decision at the School of Theology to become competent in intercultural teaching, learning, and formation to better serve our international students, who made up 26 percent of our student population. We took the Intercultural Development Inventory (IDI), sought consultation, participated in workshops, and established an Intercultural Advisory Committee. Our eyes were opened. Collectively, we were midpoint on the IDI developmental scale, which is minimization, meaning we focus on our commonalities. If we are to move to the next level on the scale, which is acceptance and adaptation, there was work to be done. The faculty needed to know about its own culture while learning about our students' cultures. It may seem paradoxical that to know others better, we must first know ourselves; yet self-awareness and self-understanding are often enhanced by our interactions with the others we are trying to understand. Moreover, efforts to understand the link between background, worldview, values, and actions begin with us as we reach out to others.

As our work on intercultural teaching and formation deepened, we began to recognize that our focus was off kilter. Initially we focused on understanding national cultures. Over time, we increasingly became aware of other intersectionalities, such as family life cycle and structure, age, gender and orientation, and varying abilities. Listening to pastoral leaders, we also added organizational culture and hierarchical culture as critical to understanding the stories of people in ministry. This was another aha moment. The difficulties in ministerial relationships, such as communication breakdowns, defensiveness, and blaming others, may in part be stirred up by cultural differences, which if understood may lead to building better, more resilient relationships. As a faculty we have a responsibility to the Church and students preparing for ministry to learn how to approach, understand, and dialogue about complex issues and across different perspectives. The one-time workshop approach needs to be replaced with ongoing, systemic, institutionally sustained opportunities for learning.

PAUSE FOR REFLECTION
- What is the most significant intersection at which you find yourself at this stage of life and ministry?
- To what extent are you invested in creating a healthy ministerial workplace?
- What do you hope to gain from this book to support you in your efforts?

ALWAYS, WE BEGIN AGAIN

Today our understanding of the ministerial workplace, those who serve it, and intercultural dynamics is quite different than when we began writing this book. Workplace health requires new cultural languages and more cultural-friendly practices if we want to be an inclusive Church. Many co-workers are not prepared to have a vibrant conversation that includes differences and listening. They continue the pattern of discourse that ends up with winners and losers.

In the early decades of lay ecclesial ministry, there was no standard human resource guide for laypeople employed by the Church. Often the pay scales for Catholic school systems were used to design salary ranges for parish lay employees. We quickly learned the term *fire at will*—when one's employment can be broken by either party without notice. The employee can resign anytime they choose, just as the employer can fire them at any time without just cause.

A shift began in earnest in 2005 when the U.S. Conference of Catholic Bishops (USCCB) issued the document *Co-workers in the Vineyard of the Lord*, the product of research and many crucial conversations. It provided a guide for dioceses, parishes, and academic institutions as they advanced development for the role of lay ecclesial ministry and ministerial formation. *Co-workers* theologically and pastorally integrated the various forms of Church ministry—lay ecclesial ministers and the ordained—as a network of ministerial relationships. This was on the heels of the National Association of Church Personnel Administrators (NACPA) developing *Church Workplace Standards: A Self-Audit* (2004), aimed at encouraging dioceses, parishes, ministerial formators, national ministerial organizations, and universities and seminaries to evaluate their ways of operating to ensure standards and best practices in creating a healthy workplace and thriving pastoral leaders.

Beginning in 2007, Saint John's School of Theology and Seminary in Collegeville, Minnesota, under the leadership of Dr. Jeff Kaster, committed itself to harnessing the intentions of *Co-workers in the Vineyard of the Lord*. Throughout the region and on a national level, Saint John's worked with pastoral leaders to explore the knowledge, skills, and opportunities for all ecclesial ministers, ordained and lay, to interpret theologically and pastorally the movement of God within the life of the Church. One result was development of a common set of standards for lay ministry for Minnesota's dioceses based on the *National Certification Standards for Lay Ecclesial Ministers* (2003), approved by the USCCB's Commission on Certification and Accreditation. Saint John's convened its first national symposium on lay ecclesial ministry in the summer of 2007, focused on the call from the bishops to study the critical issues facing lay ecclesial ministry and dialoguing about effective ways to support and advance ministry in the Church.[1]

One result of that symposium was the development of a document by the Canon Law Society of America (CLSA), "Toward Canonical Consideration of the Authorization of Lay Ecclesial Ministers for Ministry." The CLSA requested the Center for Applied Research in the Apostolate (CARA) to study how the authorization process for lay ecclesial ministry was implemented in dioceses across the United States. CARA identified seventy-five potential diocesan respondents from its database and achieved a 60 percent response. This research provided significant insights into the ministerial workplace:

- Half of responding dioceses said that at least half of their lay ecclesial ministries (LEMs) had a written job description.
- Nearly nine in ten responding dioceses said that less than a quarter of their LEMs had an official appointment to their position by the bishop.
- Just 5 percent said that most or all of their LEMs had an appointment by the bishop.

- One in five responding dioceses said that at least half of their LEMs had a contract for their position, but more than half said that less than a quarter of their LEMs operate under a contract.
- Only 21 percent of the responding dioceses had a written, periodic evaluation of lay ecclesial ministers.[2]

In 2011, a second national symposium at Saint John's focused on advancing the national will for the authorization and certification of lay ecclesial ministers and exploring more thoroughly the theology of call and vocation of the lay ecclesial minister. Saint John's brought together a team of national partners and theologians who tested their theological interpretations of ministry with the lay ecclesial ministers attending the symposium. Over months of writing and rewriting to capture a developing consensus, the results appeared in *In the Name of the Church: Vocation and Authorization of Lay Ecclesial Ministry* (Liturgical Press, 2012).

In 2015, Saint John's was a contributing partner for the Lay Ministry Summit convened by the USCCB in St. Louis. Using *Co-workers* as a framework, the summit considered various topics, including the relationship between the lay apostolate and lay ecclesial ministry, emerging pathways for culturally and generationally diverse populations, formation and authorization of lay ministers, and the state of parish workplaces, all in the context of the co-responsibility of the laity and the ordained for the work of the New Evangelization. The summit was a unique opportunity for bishops to discuss together with other leaders the state of lay ecclesial ministry today and next steps that might be considered.

A third symposium on lay ecclesial ministry was scheduled for summer of 2020. COVID intervened. We reconfigured our plan for a face-to-face event into a Zoom-based gathering of co-workers from around the country for a series of smaller events over the course of a year. Part of the work was to invite participants to engage the narratives and theological reflections presented in this book as well as address some of the key dimensions of developing and sustaining healthy ministerial workplaces.

Finally, in 2021, the National Association for Lay Ministry (NALM) called together a working group to review and revise its 2007 position paper "Working in the Vineyard: A Statement on Employment Practices for Lay Ecclesial Ministers." In the face of continuing challenges, the working group shifted the 2005 image of *Co-workers in the Vineyard of the Lord* from *vineyard* to a contemporary *field hospital*, which reflected Pope Francis's (2013) call to heal wounds and warm the hearts of the faithful (2013). The working group concluded,

> Today many in pastoral leadership find themselves simultaneously serving and needing a field hospital as wounded healers. In recent years, many lay ecclesial ministers and their co-workers experienced deep wounds. The abuse scandals have deeply affected Church employees; bankruptcies, the loss of trust, and the COVID-19 pandemic have created stressful realities. Some lay ecclesial ministers have lost their positions or have been asked to take cuts in salary due to these troubling times. And yet, often disenfranchised and even demoralized, many lay ecclesial ministers have worked to be faithful to their vocational call to serve.[3]

All these national gatherings and the literature they produced related to lay ecclesial ministry moved the principles of *Co-workers in the Vineyard of the Lord* forward. What we noticed was increasing specificity about what was required to harvest what the Church was learning about lay ministry and, more important, what it required for the ministry to thrive. In this instance, thriving is not only that lay ecclesial ministers feel recognized and affirmed. Rather, the whole life of the Church would thrive. The work ahead always called for a new sense of agency within all ministers to understand what was happening in their contexts and creating new patterns of action and relationship to respond with zeal. Cultivating such zeal is part of our purpose for this book.

IGNITING THE DIVINE SPARK

The ebb and flow of ministerial life can cause the light of zeal and commitment in even the most resilient people to flicker. Over the past decade and through the COVID pandemic, people have been through traumatic experiences. A long shadow has been cast over the vineyard. With words such as *field hospital* and *sourpusses* emerging as mirrors for self-reflection, it feels at times as though the Church is adrift. Tales abound about tensions between people who were able to work from home during the pandemic and those who were not and between those who received pay adjustments and those who did not. In *Leaders: Your Organization Needs You More Than Ever*, Michael Bush writes, "Many leaders do not know how to manage these issues, so they retreat to what they know: command and control. They are using different terminology (they have been hearing and reading a lot about empathy) but coming through their new words is an old-school approach."

Recovering the divine spark is not new to this generation of pastoral leaders. When Vincent van Gogh (1853–1890) sought ordination in the Dutch Reformed Church, he was deemed "unfit for the dignity of the priesthood." While he came to reject the lives of the clergymen, he did not lose his awareness of God's presence in the lives of the poor, nor his sense of God urging him to love others. His painting *Starry Night*, set in Arles, France, portrays his sense of the Church losing its divine spark. In the very center of the painting is a white church he imported from his childhood to create a parable of his own life. The homes surrounding the church are lit with warm light. However, the church, the other building in the painting, is completely dark. Van Gogh paints what he knows in his heart. The Spirit has left the Church but is active in nature and the community.[4]

Today, our faith communities have been called by Pope Francis to be a field hospital, to heal wounds and to warm the hearts of the faithful. Yet many in pastoral leadership find themselves simultaneously serving and needing a field hospital as wounded healers. The field hospital provides an intimate image of a Church in crisis. Pope Francis noticed this general malaise. Like the vineyard, the vine without sun withers and weakens, sometimes it dies. So too with the Church. Pope Francis has said that when Christians see more of a sourpuss that fails to communicate the joy of being loved by God, the witness of the Church suffers.[5] In the United States the workplace is now the fifth leading cause of death, writes Jeffery Pfeffer in his book *Dying for a Paycheck*. This is higher than Alzheimer's or kidney disease. Pfeffer's research shows that the mismanagement of workforces causes more than 120,000 deaths a year and accounts for 5 to 8 percent of annual healthcare costs. He cites conditions like excessive work hours, work-family conflict, lack of health insurance, and lack of control and autonomy. Pfeffer poignantly states, "According to the Mayo Clinic, the person you report to at work is more important for your health than your family doctor."[6] Church leaders must take ownership of the environment they create. For example, Angie Hong, in the article "Women of Color in Ministry Are Not Scarce, Just Unsupported," offers eight suggestions for those in Church leadership who want to do a better job of supporting women of color. One of the suggestions is to commit to the work of inclusion as an entire staff. Hong writes, "Too often, the women of color on staff care the most about anti-racism or diversity efforts, tacking extra responsibilities to lead these efforts onto their jobs. By spreading out these efforts across all staff, there can be transformation at every level. The senior leadership should take part in inclusion efforts, showing that this is essential to the Church."[7]

Today's lay ecclesial ministers are different than the ordained men and religious women who single-handedly, with the help of God, led the Church prior to the Second Vatican Council. Lay ecclesial ministers live in the trenches of contemporary life. They often come to work after a night of struggling with sleepless babies or caring for parents moving into adult living centers, while sustaining their marriage through it all. Or they are single adults who work two jobs because one job just doesn't cover their college debt repayment and their living expenses. They spend an inordinate amount of time explaining to their family and parishioners that they too have a vocation. They share the joys and burdens of Church life with their pastors. They work outside their job descriptions to be on call when the pastor is away for a weekend or an overdue vacation. They work the evening shift because that is when children, youth, and adults are available for faith formation. And they are expected to be at work the next morning at 8:30 for a staff meeting. Lay ecclesial ministers live with job insecurity because they can be fired at will. In addition, with little attention to job descriptions, employee evaluations or authorization by their bishop, they have no metric for a job well done.

LAMENT AND MOVING FORWARD

Too often, people enter a conversation on ministerial identity with what they can't do—for example, preside at celebrations of the sacraments. Such a start point is limiting. Pastoral leaders, ordained and lay alike, need to be revitalized. Brian McLaren, in *Finding Our Way Again*, writes, "When we lose our way, then we will lose our next generation, and perhaps, after a few generations we will face extinction.…How do we break the cycle into which we have fallen?"[8] During these demanding times and the need for healing, courage, and renewal, ecclesial ministers return to the ancient Christian practice of lament and hope. In Psalm 80, the psalmist describes Israel's origin as God's people in terms of a vine and comments on the sorry state of God's vine. Over time pastoral leaders become disengaged as they tire of their lack of appropriate authority, validation of their vocations, the ineffective use of their gifts, working relationships that are more transactional than transformative, and institutional roadblocks and setbacks. All of this contributes to a culture in which people do not thrive and their vocational calling is tested.

The gospel invokes a yes by exhorting us to love one another and asks people to abide in Jesus Christ (John 15:1–9). The vineyard image in the Gospel of John (John 15:1–9) insists that God remains in personal relationship with the people, continues to care for and preserve them, and stays faithful even when people fail to do so. The vineyard is an image of hope; it emphasizes God's continuing care. The problem Jesus speaks of in John 15 was not with God, the owner, or the vineyard, which is God's people. Rather, the problem was with the tenants, the leaders. God heard the cries of pain from Israel and wanted justice and right relationships, as it is written in the Gospel of Matthew: "You too go into my vineyard, and I will give you what is just" (Matt 20:4).

Who heals the wounded healer? Often, we need a reminder and perhaps support in the forms of Sabbath time to take a break from people, places, and stresses that mount. Parker Palmer encourages leaders "to be a person who takes special responsibility focusing on inside him or herself, inside his or her consciousness, lest the act of leadership create more harm than good."[9] In this pause is the safe space to explore the story behind the wound to quicken awareness as well as a desire to seeks another way, a different future, rather than just recapitulate the past. This does not necessarily mean "leaving" the Church. But it does involve a deep commitment to face into the bold challenges required to make real the hoped-for vision of how we actually work and minister together.

UNDERSTANDING BURNOUT WITHIN THE CONTEXT OF MINISTRY

The Sustaining the Ministerial Workplace project, begun in 2019, led us to define work engagement and burnout as a specific *psychological state* that identifies an underlying *motivational process*. To explore the issues of burnout in the workplace, we adopted the Maslach Burnout Inventory (MBI) and Areas of Work-Life Survey (AWS) for Human Services. These two instruments provide different ways of looking at burnout. One focuses on the individual's level of burnout and the other explores one's feelings about the organizational workplace so that mismatches can be identified.

Christina Maslach, lead researcher for the MBI-AWS inventory, is one of the foremost experts in researching work engagement, burnout, and strategies for improving one's relationship with work. The word *burnout*, writes Maslach, "evokes images of a final flickering flame, or a charred and empty shell, of dying embers and cold, gray ashes. Burnout is a syndrome of emotional exhaustion, depersonalization, and reduced personal accomplishment that can occur among individuals who do 'people-work' of some kind."[10] *Burnout* is an imprecise term for a person who is exhausted and can no longer push through a day's work or one more project. Along with this is a feeling of helplessness that "there is nothing I can do about it."

The MBI measures how frequently one feels emotional exhaustion, depersonalization, and personal accomplishment. High frequency of emotional exhaustion and depersonalization contribute to burnout, while high frequency of personal accomplishment decreases burnout. Maslach characterizes these three indicators as the following:

Emotional exhaustion. Feeling overwhelmed, stressed, and weary; the demands of the job feel far greater than one is able to give. A ministerial example is "I feel drained from my work."
Depersonalization. Lost enthusiasm or an unfeeling, impersonal response toward the recipients of one's care. The job feels like a burden or a chore. A ministerial example is "I don't really care what happens to 'those people.'"
Low personal accomplishment. Feeling low levels of competence and effectiveness, and not having a beneficial impact on people. A

ministerial example is "I really don't feel that my efforts ultimately are worthwhile."[11]

These three dimensions—individual resiliency, reactions to others on the job, and reaction to oneself on the job—influence where one finds themselves on the continuum from burnout to engagement.[12] A person who is engaged is positive and supportive and has a sense of efficacy and personal accomplishment. The person who experiences burnout typically negatively evaluates their accomplishment, and feels emotionally exhausted and uninvolved with co-workers and the community. In our research, people in ministry had an exceedingly high sense of accomplishment, with 41 percent being engaged in their work and only 7 percent experiencing burnout. Our assumption that lay ecclesial ministers were burned out was *not* accurate. What follows in the data is that the "sourpuss faces" that were observed are not simply individual problems of people working in the Church; rather they are significantly affected by the organizational environment in which they work.

Many profiles of people in ministry (lay ecclesial and ordained) indicate feelings of ineffectiveness (34 percent) or being overextended (20 percent). A minister who feels ineffective has a low sense of personal accomplishment, and diminished feelings of competence in their work that results from tedium or an environment that offers little recognition for a job well done. A minister who feels overextended typically shows a high level of emotional exhaustion. This profile is typical of one who is dedicated to their job and who derives a strong sense of accomplishment from their work yet feels emotionally exhausted due to long work hours and disrupted recovery opportunities. They are fulfilled and involved, but emotionally drained.

ELEMENTS OF THE MINISTERIAL WORKPLACE

The Area Work-Life Survey focuses on one's perception of the workplace and measures the impact of workload, control, reward, community, fairness, and values in the organization. The structure and functioning of the workplace shape people's relationship to their work, how they carry out their ministry, how they interact with other people, and ultimately what they think and feel about what they do. To the six elements of the Area Work-Life Survey, we added two other elements our ministry consultants recommended: vocation and financial well-being, because of their high significance for co-workers. Using these eight elements we can gain an advanced understanding of the ministerial workplace. The AWS focuses people's experience on specific dimensions of the workplace that extensive research confirms affect the quality of work life and provides the fullest picture possible of the situation.

In what follows, we provide Maslach's definition for the six elements used in her research and the two elements we added. After each element description, we provide a pause-for-reflection activity that invites readers to complete the index we developed as a tool for assessing healthy ministerial workplaces. After each statement, check the response that comes closest to your experience in your current setting. The full index and its use is included in the appendices.

Community: The quality of an organization's social environment. People thrive in communities characterized by support, collaboration, and positive feelings. Mismatches occur when you don't have a positive connection with others at work.[13]

TABLE 2.1: PRACTICES FOR COMMUNITY SELF-ASSESSMENT					
Practices for Community	Strongly Agree	Agree	Neither Agree nor Disagree	Disagree	Strongly Disagree
1. Open and honest communication among the staff supports and encourages me.	5	4	3	2	1
2. I work at building trust with my colleagues for effective teamwork.	5	4	3	2	1
3. I value individual differences in the workplace and take action to make all feel welcome and accepted.	5	4	3	2	1

From Field Hospital to Thriving Vineyard

4. My workplace provides opportunities for community building that supports collaboration and a positive spirit among us.	5	4	3	2	1
5. I find our regular opportunities as staff for prayer and faith-sharing ground my ministry.	5	4	3	2	1
6. I strive to cooperate with others to create and sustain a healthy workplace.	5	4	3	2	1

Control: The opportunity to make choices and decisions, to solve problems, and to fulfill job responsibilities. A good match has correspondence between control and accountability. A mismatch occurs when you lack sufficient control to fulfill your responsibilities.[14]

TABLE 2.2: PRACTICES FOR CONTROL SELF-ASSESSMENT					
Practices for Control	Strongly Agree	Agree	Neither Agree nor Disagree	Disagree	Strongly Disagree
1. I generally have adequate control over my time and resources to accomplish what is expected.	5	4	3	2	1
2. I have sufficient freedom and authority to make decisions based on the responsibilities of my job description.	5	4	3	2	1
3. I think our patterns of cooperation as a team are effective and integrated.	5	4	3	2	1

Continued

4. I am able to use processes in place to resolve conflicts and concerns.	5	4	3	2	1
5. I have enough discretion in my work to exercise innovation and creativity in the face of changes that are emerging in ministry.	5	4	3	2	1

Fairness: The extent to which the organization has consistent and equitable rules for everyone, and that resources are allocated according to generally understood and consistent procedures. Fairness communicates respect for the organization's members. A lack of fairness indicates confusion in an organization's values and in its relationships with people.[15]

TABLE 2.3: PRACTICES FOR FAIRNESS SELF-ASSESSMENT					
Practices for Fairness	Strongly Agree	Agree	Neither Agree nor Disagree	Disagree	Strongly Disagree
1. I find that our processes and policies are fair to all employees and volunteers.	5	4	3	2	1
2. I contribute to shaping expectations and assumptions about how work gets done.	5	4	3	2	1
3. The annual review process contributes positively to my ongoing development.	5	4	3	2	1
4. I am equipped to recruit, select, form and evaluate volunteers.	5	4	3	2	1
5. I believe that my workplace operates in a way that does not discriminate in regard to race, ethnicity, national origin, gender, orientation, disability and language preferences.	5	4	3	2	1

Reward: Financial and social recognition for contributions on the job. A meaningful reward system acknowledges your contributions to work and provides clear indications of what the organization values.

People experience a lack of recognition as devaluing their work and themselves.[16]

TABLE 2.4: PRACTICES FOR REWARD SELF-ASSESSMENT

Practices for Reward	Strongly Agree	Agree	Neither Agree nor Disagree	Disagree	Strongly Disagree
1. My ministry offers me a sense of personal and professional satisfaction.	5	4	3	2	1
2. I am given opportunities to discern how to develop and apply my gifts in new, life-giving ways.	5	4	3	2	1
3. Due to the complexity of my position(s) I have flexibility in scheduling, prioritizing assignments, and in collaborating with others.	5	4	3	2	1
4. My supervisor and colleagues recognize my contributions to our common work.	5	4	3	2	1
5. I feel appreciated.	5	4	3	2	1
6. In peak cycles I can depend on others to assist.	5	4	3	2	1

Workload: The amount of work to be done in a given time. A manageable workload provides the opportunity to do what you enjoy, to pursue career objectives, and to develop professionally. A crisis in workload is not just stretching to meet a new challenge but going beyond human limits.[17]

TABLE 2.5: PRACTICES FOR WORKLOAD SELF-ASSESSMENT

Practices for Workload	Strongly Agree	Agree	Neither Agree nor Disagree	Disagree	Strongly Disagree
1. My workload is reasonable, enabling me to meet the expectations for my position.	5	4	3	2	1

Continued

2. My responsibilities in my ministry are commensurate with my skills and credentials.	5	4	3	2	1
3. My workload is outlined in a clearly stated job/role description.	5	4	3	2	1
4. My workload enables me to set appropriate boundaries around my time and priorities.	5	4	3	2	1
5. I have sufficient opportunities annually for personal and professional development that my ministry site actively supports.	5	4	3	2	1

Values: Values are what is important to you and the organization. When personal and organizational values are congruent, successes are shared. Mismatches occur when differences exist between your values and the organization's values, or if the organization does not practice its stated values.[18]

TABLE 2.6: PRACTICES FOR VALUES SELF-ASSESSMENT					
Practices for Values	Strongly Agree	Agree	Neither Agree nor Disagree	Disagree	Strongly Disagree
1. The values that guide my practice of ministry align with the stated values we profess in our workplace.	5	4	3	2	1
2. I integrate the stated values of our workplace in my daily ministry.	5	4	3	2	1
3. Scripture and theology form and inform the way I minister.	5	4	3	2	1

4. I am able to receive feedback when the way I minister does not align with values.	5	4	3	2	1
5. I feel safe giving feedback when actions or decisions do not align with values.	5	4	3	2	1

Financial Well-Being: Financial stability enables lay ecclesial ministers to balance day-to-day, month-to-month personal finances, and absorb a financial shock. Instability creates fear and worry about making ends meet, healthcare, and retirement.

TABLE 2.7: PRACTICES FOR FINANCIAL WELL-BEING SELF-ASSESSMENT					
Practices for Financial Well-Being	Strongly Agree	Agree	Neither Agree nor Disagree	Disagree	Strongly Disagree
1. I have adequate financial resources to fulfill the vision of the ministry.	5	4	3	2	1
2. I am aware the salary for my position is a just and competitive salary.	5	4	3	2	1
3. I have adequate training to manage the budgetary responsibilities for my ministry.	5	4	3	2	1
4. The budgeting process is clear and provides opportunities for input.	5	4	3	2	1
5. My benefits package is wholistic, including provisions for ongoing professional and spiritual growth.	5	4	3	2	1
6. I can provide decently for my own needs and those of my family.	5	4	3	2	1

Vocation: Recognition and active support for the vocational call of ministry formed in prayer, service, and study furthers a sense of personal satisfaction and positively impacts the ministerial organization. Lack of recognition, especially of the vocational character of lay ecclesial ministry, is experienced as demeaning and degrading.

TABLE 2.8: PRACTICES FOR VOCATION SELF-ASSESSMENT					
Practices for Vocation	Strongly Agree	Agree	Neither Agree nor Disagree	Disagree	Strongly Disagree
1. Workplace leadership actively recognizes what I do as a ministerial vocation.	5	4	3	2	1
2. I continue to feel called by God and the community to the work with which I am entrusted.	5	4	3	2	1
3. My position calls me to use my greatest gifts and skills to serve the people of God.	5	4	3	2	1
4. My workplace and those I serve support and affirm me as a person in my ministerial vocation.	5	4	3	2	1
5. I am open to new movements of the Spirit in my vocation.	5	4	3	2	1

Weaving and strengthening the fabric of community is a collective effort and starts with a shift in mindset about our connectedness. Peter Block writes in *Community: The Structure of Belonging*, "What makes community building so complex is that it occurs in an infinite number of small steps, sometimes in quiet moments that we notice out of the corner of our eye. It calls for us to treat as important many things that we thought were incidental. An afterthought becomes the point; a comment made in passing defines who we are more than all that came before it.…It gets down to this: How are we going to be when we gather?"[19] These eight elements are not exclusive of all possible factors affecting a healthy workplace. They do represent key aspects to which we can attend that will make a difference. They contribute to a sense of common purpose, a sense of community as Block defines it, in which we consciously and intentionally decide how we will gather.

BEYOND THE FIELD HOSPITAL

The work initiated by this project and its insights hold the possibility of creating something new. We decide if we want a future that has qualities of meaning and purpose that we choose to live for. What do we want to stand for? Naming the possibilities provides a new entrance to our ministerial relationships and workplace. The possibility enters with us.

What does this require of us? Certainly, we are reminded that we are called "to do justice, and love goodness, and to walk humbly with your God" (Mic 6:8). Listening to the stories of co-workers over the years and engaging the stories written for this book by eight experienced lay ecclesial ministers have caused a shift in perspective for us. We can no longer dwell in the land of complaint. We respect the need to name truthfully and accurately what needs to change and how the resistance to needed change harms individuals and comprises the mission of the gospel. As we argue for a deeper understanding of intercultural communication, how our differences intersect, we see in fresh ways the bounty of ancient Christian practices and the animating gifts of the Holy Spirit. Each of us has the capacity and power to risk an encounter that brings peace and calm, healing, and love.

The work of those concerned about the vitality of ministry and the well-being of all the Church's ministers begins by increasing self-awareness and individual consciousness while building a covenant culture where collectively we become whole. Each of us must examine our own role in the system, look at the way we have fostered unity or division, explore our implicit biases, and reflect on times we have avoided connections with others who are different, or put up with systems that do not seek the well-being of all. "If we engage in the collective without some practice of individual consciousness, we're more likely to get caught up in group think and only use a fraction our human capacity. Without consciousness, there is no choice," writes Claudia Horwitz, an activist and founder of Stone Circles.[20]

The mix of people with varying perspectives, understandings, and expectations that make up any Church or ministry staff contributes to the complexity of ministry. Navigating them at times will be uncomfortable. Discomfort, however, is an element in the change process. It can cause us to withdraw from the fray, keep our heads down, and just do our job. On the other hand, as we grow in self-awareness and welcome what we learn as we embrace our differences as sources of learning, we become agents of the change we have been waiting for. Everyone shares responsibility for developing a thriving and engaging workplace. In the next chapter, we offer ways to better understand that challenge and the opportunities it holds.

Chapter 3

BEYOND THE SINGLE STORY

FROM DEFENSIVENESS TO DIFFERENCES

This book centers around the experiences of eight seasoned lay ecclesial ministers facing workplace challenges. Each narrative describes the writer's interaction with another—perhaps a supervisor, co-worker, parishioner, or the system. These ministers represent a range of social identities, including race, gender, educational background, ministerial experience, life development, married and single, and allies for the LGBTQ+ community. They bring all this to how they tell their stories about one aspect of organizational culture: community, fairness, financial well-being, reward, control, values, vocation, or workload. Each story sheds light on personal maneuvers, interplay among co-workers, and institutional reactions. Sometimes the stories are gnarly because they tap into nearly visceral encounters that writers can still recall vividly. In telling their stories, they lay bare their own cultural identities, beliefs, values, and attitudes that trigger deep emotions and form subgroups, often unknowingly.

As important as these eight narratives have been to this book, they are not definitive descriptions of the ministerial workplace; other ministers may tell the story differently. Indeed, Chimamanda Ngozi Adichie cautions against relying on single stories, writing that "the single story [or perspective] creates stereotypes, and the problem with stereotypes is not that they are untrue, but that they are incomplete. They make one story become the only story."[1] Stories are effective ways to educate and create the all-important aha moment that enlightens people. The stories may tug on one's heartstrings or recall a related experience. Biases and assumptions may be interrupted by a surprising twist that creates cognitive dissonance for the reader.

In this chapter we examine the dynamics of sustaining a healthy ministerial workplace considering the frame shift that occurred for us and was introduced in the previous chapter. Exploring social identity, national and organizational cultures, and personality traits helps us understand how unexamined differences can be obstacles to effective teamwork and a staff's shared commitment to advance the message of the gospel. We will examine how our differences shape our hearts, minds, and behaviors and influence the health of workplace structures. Understanding these differences more deeply enables us to leverage their potential for creativity and collaboration.

Our goal in this chapter is to establish an understanding of culture within the contextual practice of ministry. To accomplish that we will invite readers to reflect on their personal, social, and cultural identities, beliefs, values, and attitudes and how they affect one's sense of self and interactions with others. Effectively ministering across our differences requires *cultural humility*, a concept we will return to frequently. Cultural humility is a disposition to put yourself in the place of another person, whether they be stranger or co-worker. It flows from increased self-awareness and from taking ownership of one's strengths and limitations. We provide tools and activities that aid in developing cultural humility.

DIMENSIONS OF CULTURE

In chapter 2 we defined *culture* as the changing set of shared and implicit values, attitudes, practices, and systems of meaning that characterize a group of people and help them make sense of the world. In other words, it is "a pattern of thinking, feeling, and reacting to the various situations and actions."[2] Culture is the collective programming of the mind that distinguishes the members of one group from another.[3] The way a group of people solve problems and reconcile dilemmas is also culture.[4]

Culture expresses itself in myriad forms, and no culture is objectively better or worse, superior or inferior, to another. People and systems are complex. An important lesson as we become better observers of our workplace cultures is that it is presumptive to assume we know its culture based on what we can visibly see. Moreover, throughout our lives and in our ministerial work we find ourselves at the intersection of many cultures. Every culture has frameworks and patterns that prompt questions and raise issues. They carry a set of unwritten rules that distinguish the members of one group from another. In addition, most people belong to several different groups at the same time that unavoidably have different perspectives.

Cultural difference is something each of us is reflexively aware of when we find ourselves saying in certain situations, "That's not how I would do it," or when we are surprised at our ignorance when we finally recognize, "It didn't occur to me *they* might feel that way." Culture is what makes a group an "us" as opposed to a "them." In any intercultural encounter, when tension arises, there is always a temptation to feel that others are simply wrong or have faulty intentions rather than to realize that they are acting according to different rules. When behaviors are interpreted outside their cultural context, those behaviors are usually inaccurately interpreted and result in misunderstanding and inappropriate responses that in turn can lead to conflict.

Because of the complexity of culture, this work is ambitious. Figure 3.1 sets the stage for the lens we are using to interpret the ministerial workplace and strengthen our ability to engage in conversations around differences. Tools and activities will be provided for individual self-awareness and group dialogue.

Figure 3.1: Primary Lens of Culture

National culture and organizational culture are two sources of differences and provide a way to understand the day-to-day interactions of co-workers in their workplace. Values rooted in national culture are passed from generation to generation and internalized by a child's tenth birthday. They can change over time because of outside influences that require accommodation, but they cannot be changed simply by one person's plan or by political, religious, or academic edict. National culture is the fundamental material with which we work. Organizational culture is established in the workplace and reflects the attitude about "how we do things around here." Organizational culture is more readily changed due to changes in leadership, composition of the workforce, and social or institutional shifts.

To strengthen our ability to minister across differences, it is important to become more aware of the cultural lenses we use and how they affect our perspective. Awareness and curiosity, then, increase our capacity to see from the perspective of another person. Understanding cultural values of others *does not* allow one to predict group "behavior" and responses with certainty. At the same time, a working knowledge of how people of a cultural group generally think and behave provides a useful starting point for navigating intercultural interaction and differences.

There are two theories that are particularly helpful in developing a broader understanding of culture and, with it, a disposition for cultural humility: the iceberg theory and cultural dimensions theory.

LAYERS OF CULTURE: WHAT WE SEE, WHAT WE DON'T

Icebergs are disproportionate in terms of what we actually see. The top 10 percent is visible, but 90 percent of their mass is below the surface. Culture is similar. Anthropologist Edward Hall developed the **iceberg model** to capture the power dimensions in groups and organizations.[5] First published in the 1970s, Hall's model also provides a way to envision the breadth and complexity of human cultures. When first interacting with a new culture, maybe through an immersion experience at multicultural celebrations, one encounters through one's senses things like food, music, visual arts, language, celebrations, and games.

These things matter. They are the visible and tangible ways any culture maintains its sense of identity and unity. However, even these visible signs of a culture can be fluid. Recipes, games, and arts can change over time. Even language shifts with each generation. The cultural facets of the top 10 percent of the iceberg have relatively low emotional load. They matter to people, but they can also be changed and altered without fundamentally challenging the very core of a culture or people's ideas about who they are.

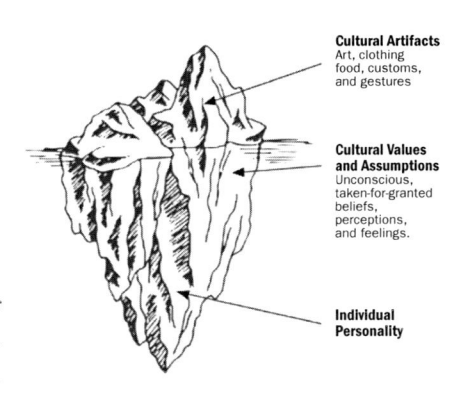

Cultural Artifacts
Art, clothing food, customs, and gestures

Cultural Values and Assumptions
Unconscious, taken-for-granted beliefs, perceptions, and feelings.

Individual Personality

This above-surface culture is what we see when we're introduced to a new group of people, but it's figuratively just the tip of the iceberg. When we dip below the surface, things get more intense. In Hall's model, this is part of the 90 percent of culture that remains below the surface, and it can be divided into two categories: unspoken rules and values.

The first are the unspoken rules of a society that include things like shared work ethic, identity, view of authority, nonverbal communication, how people interact or show emotions, concepts of personal space, definitions of beauty, and basic ideas about manners and behavior. This more hidden part of a culture takes more time for an outsider to understand. What is below the waterline of culture also carries a heavier emotional load.

The second are values that ultimately define a culture and carry the greatest emotional load. Here is where people get their ideas about childrearing, definitions of adulthood, concepts of self, roles of gender/sex/age/class, kinship and family networks, pace of work, and the tempo of society. People will actively resist changing these values because they define how they see and interpret the world. Formed in a culture, people "just know" what is good and bad, right and wrong, and acceptable or unacceptable behavior.[6] When these anchoring values begin to change, people feel threatened because their identity is at stake. To be clear, the goal is not to change another person but to become aware of differences and respect how people view the world. Hall expressed it this way: "Most of culture lies hidden outside voluntary control, making up the warp and weft of human existence. It penetrates to the roots of [an individual's] nervous system and determines how he perceives the world. Even when small fragments of culture are elevated to awareness, they are difficult to change."[7]

At the very bottom of the iceberg are an individual's unique personality traits and experiences, charisms and gifts, strengths, personality traits such as introversion and extroversion, favorite foods, and so on. Two graduate students can go through the same ministerial formation program, yet they will engage differently in the same ministry, relative to their unique personality.

Barbara was in her first parish position in the late 1980s. She was responsible for the Rite of Christian Initiation of Adults (RCIA) process already in place and familiar with it because she attended it a few years earlier when she was becoming Catholic. As a freshly minted lay ecclesial minister with a master's degree in pastoral ministry, however, she was different than the person the pastor knew previously as a volunteer youth minister. When Barbara asked the pastor if he wanted to meet and go over the process for the evening, he declined and said he and the associates would be there to greet the people. He asked Barbara to prepare refreshments and the room, which she did in addition to organizing the process for the evening's inquiry period for the RCIA. Part of the spillover from her previous participation in the RCIA was that the pastor used a small catechism with questions and answers. Since then, Barbara had learned a new way and intended to use it to facilitate the RCIA process that evening.

While a fledgling in ministry, Barbara had confidence in what she had learned about the RCIA. As director of religious education, she put herself on the agenda as the one to first welcome the inquirers because she felt she and the priests were a team. When the pastor arrived, he grabbed a cookie and told Barbara how nice the room looked. He was pleased with the number of inquirers present and rehearsed how the evening would go. Barbara listened and quickly realized it was the "way he always did it." He had not looked at her agenda and was unprepared for a different model. This was a moment of reckoning for Barbara, who admits being tempted to "go along to get along." But she trusted the relationship she and the pastor had built over the years. As she showed him the agenda, she explained that the evening was about storytelling and learning what questions the inquirers would bring. Further, she suggested that because it was more process than content driven, any or all four of them could facilitate the evening. In a flash, the pastor said, "Let's try it the way you have outlined." The evening went well.

What is visible in this vignette is the identified roles—pastor, associates, and director of religious education. They were ordained and lay ecclesial ministers; there were varying levels of experience among them, male and female, with one person born in Ireland and native-born Americans. Clearly, the priests were the identified leaders for the evening as people lined up to introduce themselves to the pastor and his associates. Barbara tried not to take up too much space that evening, knowing the team was not of equals but still wanting to test the waters. Both the pastor and Barbara were quietly confronted that evening with who was in charge. He never lost an ounce of power that evening, and he gained some gratitude for empowering her to use her gifts and position. Not to be fooled, she knew that just under the surface, shifting leadership for the evening could have gone bad quickly and may not work in changed circumstances.

This iceberg model of culture helps illustrate why some cultural changes are so dramatic while others seem far less so. A change to the top of the iceberg will not necessarily impact what's below the surface. Most of the time, those changes are a result of deeper changes in the core values that take time to manifest in any observable way. However, if the core of the iceberg is ever greatly shaken, the impact reverberates throughout the entire iceberg.

REFLECTION FOR PAUSE
- Recall a social interaction with another person that was awkward or strained.
- What do you find hard to relate to? Draw an iceberg that describes what you know to be true about yourself.
- What is visible?
- What was unseen below the waterline?
- What are your unspoken rules?
- What are you learning about yourself?

DIMENSIONS OF CULTURE: OBSERVATION AND INTERPRETATION

Pastoral leaders working in multicultural settings must think carefully about how to motivate people, how to approach learning, and how to recruit leaders. In 1980 Geert Hofstede developed the *cultural dimensions theory* to distinguish different dimensions of national culture as a way to interpret dynamic, culture-based interactions. While culture is complex, it is not chaotic; there are clearly defined patterns to be discovered. Hofstede identified six dimensions that help explain what is happening within and between national cultures. In what follows, readers will be invited to consider how these dimensions express themselves in their lives and the values they hold. For each dimension, we indicate countries that hold these values. You can also note your personal orientation and those of another national culture.[8]

Individualism/Collectivism: The degree to which individuals are expected to look after themselves or remain loyal and integrated into groups. Collectivism is trusting the community with a decision that affects our lives. It is more than getting one another's input.[9]

Individualist	Collectivist
· Emphasis on "I"	· Emphasis on "We"
· Independence/Personal autonomy	· Relational interdependence
· Self-directed	· Group-motivated
· Individual rights and needs	· Group rights and needs
· Individual responsibility	· Accountability to the group
· Voluntary reciprocity	· Obligatory reciprocity
· Core Value: Individual freedom	· Core Value: Group harmony
USA, Australia, France	Guatemala, Peru, China, Mexico

PAUSE FOR REFLECTION
- Where is your ministerial workplace on this continuum of individualism versus collectivism?
- In what ways do you see your ministry as your work or the work of the community?

Power Distance: This is the degree to which members of a society accept differences in power and authority. In societies with high power distance, people are more likely to accept that power inequality to be appropriate and normal. There are a variety of above-the-waterline artifacts that can serve as cues to the degree of hierarchy existing within a cultural context. For example, how one is introduced to the pastor, and what the office setup suggests about power dynamics.[10]

Low Power Distance	High Power Distance
· Emphasis on equal distance · Individual achievement · Informality · Subordinates expect consultation · Self-initiative and decision-making · Willing to question and challenge the views of superiors · Core Value: Equality between people	· Emphasis on power distance · Seniority, age, rank, title · Formality · Subordinates expect direction · Obedience · Expects power builders to be entitled to privilege · Core Value: Respect for status
Israel, Costa Rica, USA	Guatemala, Russia, Mexico, China

PAUSE FOR REFLECTION
- To what degree does the ministry setting where you serve value hierarchy?
- How does that compare with your own leadership preference?

Uncertainty Avoidance: Risk is a value associated with the degree to which "a culture tolerates uncertainty and ambiguity. At one end of the spectrum are cultures that are tight, or low in risk taking or uncertainty avoidance. As much as possible, people in these cultures try to control the unexpected through safety and security measures and strict laws. On the other end of the risk value are loose cultures where ambiguity and unpredictability are welcome. Strict laws and rules are resisted, and people are more accepting of opinions different from theirs."[11]

Weak Uncertainty Avoidance	Strong Uncertainty Avoidance
· Provide few rules, little structure, and few guidelines. Tolerate unstructured and unpredictable situations. · Uncertainty is a normal feature of life, and each day is accepted as it comes. · What is different is curious. · Few and general laws or unwritten rules · Teachers may say, "I don't know." · Fast acceptance of new products and technologies · Core value: Exploration	· Prefer written rules, structure, and guidelines. · The uncertainty inherent in life is a continuous threat that must be fought. · What is different is dangerous. · Many and precise laws or unwritten rules · Teachers are supposed to have all the answers. · Hesitancy toward new products and technologies. · Core value: Certainty
Jamaica, Denmark, China, USA	Guatemala, Turkey, Brazil

PAUSE FOR REFLECTION
- Which of these tendencies do you embrace?
- How do these, the low and the high, reflect the Reign of God?

Long-Term/Short-Term Orientation: Related to the choice of focus for people's efforts: the future or the present and past. "Churches oriented to the past often had a period or perceived success known as the 'glory days,' and as a result, old-timers in the Church continue to look back longingly, remembering what it was like back then."[12]

Long-Term Orientation	Short-Term Orientation
· Fostering of virtues oriented toward future rewards · Persistence · Thrift · Ordering relationships by status and observing that order · Having a sense of shame · Core Value: Long-term benefits	· Fostering of virtues related to the past and present · Respect for tradition · Preservation of "face" · Personal steadiness and stability · Fulfilling social obligations · Core Value: Saving face
South Korea, Taiwan, Switzerland	Ghana, Columbia, USA

PAUSE FOR REFLECTION
- Are you most concerned with the past, the present, or the future right now?
- How might that shape the way you interact in the various cultures you regularly encounter?

Achievement/Nurturance: Achievement is the cultural value "that measures the importance given to action. Achievement cultures value results and materialism. Nurturance cultures value relationships and quality of life."[13]

Achievement (Doing)	Nurturance (Being)
· Emotional gender roles are distinct. · Doing · Preference for achievement, heroism, assertiveness, and material rewards for success · Work is an acceptable excuse to neglect the family (but not vice versa). · Father deals with facts; mother with feelings. · Okay for girls to cry, but boys should not; okay for boys to fight, but girls should not · Core Value: Winning	· Little to no distinction between emotional gender roles · Being · Preference for cooperation, modesty, caring for the weak, and quality of life · People try to balance family and work. · Both mother and father deal with facts and feelings. · Okay for boys and girls to cry; neither should fight · Core Value: Caring for the weak
USA, Austria, India	Israel, Brazil, Sweden

PAUSE FOR REFLECTION
- What impact does a doing and being culture have on your personhood and identities?

Direct/Indirect Communication Orientation: Direct communication refers to "instructions that specifically state and direct an action, whereas indirect communication relies on input and understanding."[14]

Indirect Communication	Direct Communication
· Emphasizes roles and implicit understanding · Values indirect conversation	· Emphasizes explicit words · Values direct communication
Brazil, East Africa, Thailand	USA, Israel, Australia

PAUSE FOR REFLECTION
Think about the cultural context of your ministerial workplace.
- Are people mostly drawn to stories and experiences or to research and statistics?
- To which are you drawn?

The dimensions of cultural values are evident in our ministerial workplaces in a variety of ways. When people are interacting with one another across cultures in which they have been formed, their cultural values could make them say or do things that are misperceived as intentional affronts or hostile.[15] Consider the example of a pastoral leadership team with diverse cultural backgrounds as they express their *attitudes, behaviors, and expectations about the new pastor appointed to their parish*. Here are possible responses applying Hofstede's cultural values dimensions:[16]

- *Collectivist*: Our pastor will provide for our Church, families, and for us.
- *Individualist*: I will work hard because he might recognize my achievements and help me get ahead.
- *High Power*: He is our father. We respect and obey him, and he looks after us.
- *Low Power*: He should listen to us and be resourceful.
- *Strong Uncertainty Avoidance*: The pastor offers stability and is technically competent.
- *Weak Uncertainty Avoidance*: He listens and has good judgment.
- *Long-Term Orientation*: The pastor knows where the parish is headed.
- *Short-Term Orientation*: He is outgoing and knows how to meet deadlines.

- *Achievement*: He is our hero. He should be tough and decisive.
- *Nurturance*: He is a person just like everybody else. He should care for the weaker among us.
- *Direct Communication*: He will do his homework before a meeting and be prepared to answer our questions.
- *Indirect Communication*: The pastor will preach the gospel and touch the hearts of people.

People from different national cultures and varying social identities have different social rules. When you communicate with people without knowing the differences, you will likely misattribute at least some aspects of their behavior. You will find meaning where none was intended, or you will miss meaning where it was intended. On the other hand, be aware that not all behaviors can be explained through national culture. There are always many factors in addition to culture that contribute to a particular course of events. These include personalities of people involved, things that happened in the recent past, longevity in the organization, and unforeseen situational variables.[17]

LEARNING THROUGH DIFFERENCES, ACROSS DIFFERENCES

Whether working alongside someone of another gender, welcoming a new co-worker or pastor, or making a pastoral visit to a ministry on the margin, we regularly navigate cultural differences. A common pitfall is a lack of awareness of our own cultural context and the unspoken rules by which we live and minister. When we are unaware of cultural differences in ministry, we can cause unintended offense, break trust, and hurt our ability to be effective ministers of the gospel.

This extensive discussion of culture is critical to figuring out what we can do when in the midst of all the differences represented in a group. A focal point for learning in the face of difference is social identity. It comprises several core concepts that we will begin exploring and mapping in this chapter. The framework for ministry across differences comes from the Center of Creative Leadership, in its book *Leading across Differences* (2010).[18] We adapted it for a hierarchical structure.

Social identity is the group(s) to which people belong based on shared characteristics such as gender, religion, race, class, sexuality, and abilities.[19]

Cultural values are the common beliefs, practices, symbols, social norms, and personal values in a society that give it a degree of coherence.[20]

Spillover is the process by which social identity differences or what happens in the family or society at large influence organizational dynamics.[21]

Triggers can be actions or series of actions that are perceived as inequity, inequality, or biases related to a social identity, and is noticeable. For an event to be a trigger, at least two members from the same identity group attribute the event or action to their social identity or the social identity group of the other party.[22] For example, a woman's treatment over a work issue triggers a sense of unfairness because her supervisor is male and does not seem to treat men in the organization in the same way.

Fault lines are dynamics in a group composed of multiple demographic attributes that can potentially subdivide a group. Fault lines may or may not be active in an organization, but they are always present. Fault lines may form along attributes such as gender, race, age, religion, nationality, or other demographic factors.[23]

IDENTITIES

In the Gospel of John, Jesus ponders the question, "Who do you say that I am?" Jesus reveals his many identities by saying he is "the bread of life" (John 6:35), "the light of the world" (John 8:12), "the gate for the sheep" (John 10:7–9), "the good shepherd" (John 10:11), "the resurrection and the life" (John 11:25), and "the true vine" (John 15:1–5). Each of these identities gives him power. Our identities can give us power or limit our power, depending on whether the cultural context is dominant or marginalized. In Activity 1 readers can uncover their various identities. Some are given at birth like gender or ethnicity or emerged in childhood like the correct use of table manners or respect toward elders. Others are chosen, like educational achievement or type of work; and some are personal and often make one feel special or unique, such as particular talents, athletic ability, or style of dressing. They are primarily intrapersonal and connect to our individual interests and expectations. Some will change over the course of a lifetime; others may remain constant. Elements of one's core personal identity may include traits, strengths and gifts, behaviors, beliefs, and skills.

Self-awareness and knowing one's own identities are essential to ministering across differences. Moving through these self-awareness activities will likely heighten a human tendency to divide people into two groups—those with commonalities and those with differences. Typically, it creates a "them" and "us" mentality. For those who interpret another through their own lens, they are using a monocultural lens: you don't do it the way I do. This monocultural lens relies on one's typical way of seeing, therefore making another person—a "them"—seem less knowledgeable, less sensitive, right, or normal compared to us. This narrowness heightens as we witness the greater diversification of parishes and staffs in which everyone is no longer from the same national culture. Consider how all this intensifies as parishes undergo some form of restructuring.

In staff development workshops we have done, participants often lament that they are siloed and don't work well together. People's workloads are heavy, and work is typically added without anything taken away. When siloes arise, they prevent community building and seem to strengthen the "us" and "them" divide between co-workers. In one instance, a staff was working hard to discover what was hopeful in their challenges with one another rather than feeling hostage to their differences. In the discussion, they recognized that they were only able to do the ministry they could do because of the many silos, which they defined as the distinct areas of work assigned to individuals. Every ministry was essential to the mission of this parish and the emerging cluster. What was needed was action that kept the distinction of their ministries from operating in isolation from one another. This new understanding turned them toward an "us," a team of co-workers. The isolating effect of silos can happen in other ways. For instance, when a person loses the opportunity to advance "their" agenda, they keep pushing back usually at the expense of another person. Polarization results. While the person's ideas may be valuable and resourceful, he or she may forget to pause and suspend judgment to gain a perspective on the whole picture.

When we take steps toward understanding differences, then, we see through an intercultural lens because we have practiced what we introduced earlier as cultural humility. National Institutes of Health defines *cultural humility* as a "a lifelong process of self-reflection and self-critique whereby the individual not only learns about another but starts with an examination of his/her own beliefs and cultural identities."[24] Victor's development of cultural humility was spurred by an experience he had as a co-trainer for a community leadership retreat designed for Minnesota reservation communities. The first time he was involved, he realized—on the second of five days—that he was the only white person among the thirty-two people in the room. He commented on this to his training partner, an Ojibwa woman, who just looked at him until he realized how odd it was to only acknowledge that in the second day of the retreat. Finally, she said, "And how does that feel?"

Cultural humility invites us to be curious about another by listening with the ear of our heart. Cultural humility can also lead to the development of crucial skills such as empathy, consensus building, servant leadership, constructive conflict management, and how to decrease prejudices and increase tolerance. In Victor's case, it was not so much issues of intolerance or prejudice, but how his cultural assumptions obscured his ability to really see the group of natives with whom he was spending time. He had centered himself. A culturally humble orientation to the web of differences can open up to learning that is rich, inspirational, and reflective of the intense creativity of a compassionate God.

Activity 1: Exploring Identities

We hope that by encouraging you to begin the process of exploring your cultural identities you will develop natural tendencies to be interested and curious about your cultural experiences as well as the cultural experiences of others. In this exercise, readers map their identities and reflect on them to explore how these identities might influence their ability to minister effectively across differences. Use the following steps to complete the maps in figure 3.2:

1. In the **cultural identity map**, write words that describe your *cultural identity*—the attributes or conditions over which you had no choice. They were given, such as nationality, race, first language, age, gender, sexual orientation, physical characteristics, certain family roles, religion or spiritual orientation, physical, emotional, development (dis)abilities, and socioeconomic status.

2. In the **social identity map**, list aspects of your *chosen identity*, including your vocation, education, hobbies, community involvement, political affiliation, where you live, certain family roles, and religious affiliation.
3. In the **core personal identity map**, write your core personal attributes—traits, behaviors, beliefs, values, strengths, gifts and skills, travels, hobbies, favorite music, movie, or food that you think make you unique as an individual. Select things that are relatively enduring about you or that are key to who you are today.

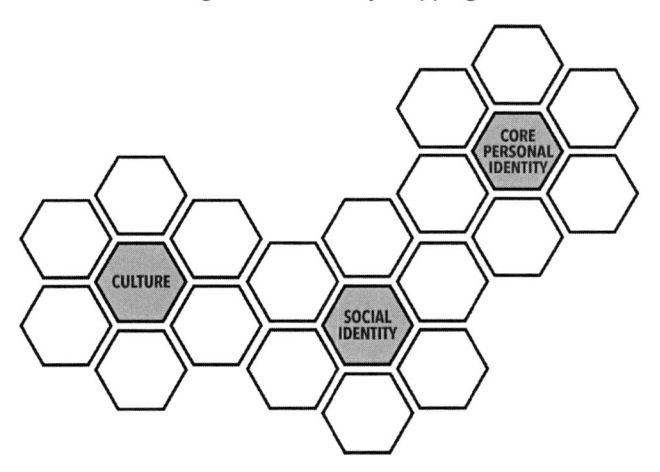

Figure 3.2: Identity Mapping

PAUSE FOR REFLECTION
- Which identities do you believe contribute to your ability to lead and minister effectively in your ministerial workplace? Which ones detract? How might they vary in how they affect your leadership and ministerial ability, depending on context?
- As a co-worker, what are things you have in common with other people in the ministerial workplace? What are things that only you or a very small number of people possess? What are the leadership implications?
- What aspects of your identity helps you make connections with people at work? What aspects of your identity get in the way?

- Are there aspects of your identity that you keep hidden—ones that are below the waterline of the iceberg? What impact might that have on you and those around you?
- How might you reveal or emphasize elements of your identity at work to build or improve relationships?
- What identities do you have that are dominant?

Activity 2: Explore Fundamental Cultural Values

Values are a culture's standard for discerning what is good and just in society. They are deeply embedded and critical for transmitting and teaching a culture's beliefs. Typically, they are established by ten years of age through our families, schools, community, and national culture. In the center of figure 3.3, write your own name. In each of the outer hexagons, write a group that has had a significant impact on your life values (examples: family, Church, a childhood organization such as Girl/Boy Scouts, Future Farmers of America, 4-H, Little League, being a first-generation American, or other significant factors in the country or region where you live or grew up). Next to each hexagon, write at least two values that you learned from that group (for example, if one circle says 4-H, values related to being a part of this group for you might be "respect for the land" or "ability to connect with neighbors"). After adding your values, look at whether there are any values that may conflict with one another. If there are, how have you managed to cope with these conflicts? Underline the three cultural groups or values that you feel are most relevant in your ministerial setting, that is, which most impact your work as a pastoral leader.

Figure 3.3: Diverse Cultural Values

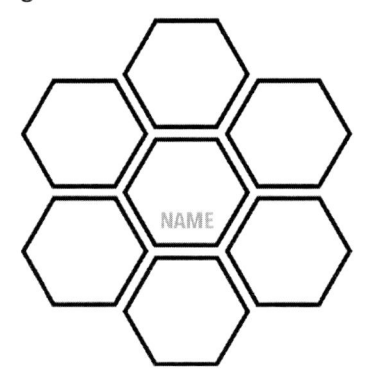

PAUSE FOR REFLECTION
- What insight have you gained about yourself from this exercise?

Spillover

Co-workers in ministry are experiencing an unprecedented time as many cultural influences and organizational dynamics escalate the need for more sensitivity, instruction, and cultural humility. Otherwise, seemingly unrelated events can have a ripple effect on other systems. First, a significant impetus to our own work in this book was the death of George Floyd, a Black man, who died after being handcuffed and pinned to the ground by Minneapolis police officers. It was captured on video, touching off a nationwide protest. For us as a faculty at Saint John's, it demanded more than another letter acknowledging our remorse about structural racism and the promise to do better. We were called to deeper conversations around issues such as diversity, equity, inclusion, and justice. To assess our readiness, we incorporated the Intercultural Development Inventory to help us understand our ability for intercultural practices and ministries. We discovered people typically overestimate their ability to use an intercultural lens to explore differences. The Intercultural Development Inventory often jumpstarts conversations that probe familiar assumptions and biases we carry about our attitudes toward differences.

Second, the Great Resignation, "quiet quitting," and antiwork sentiments are on the rise as people shift priorities and seek new opportunities that provide more autonomy, flexibility, and control over their lives, and better pay and benefits. Third, the ethnic diversity landscape is shifting. In a 2019 study, "Open Wide the Doors to Christ: A Study of Catholic Social Innovation for Parish Vitality," Marti Jewell and Mark Mogilka called for cultural sensitivity and competency training for both Anglo and Hispanic leaders. They report, "There is a need to be sensitive to the deep variety of cultures present, both within and beyond the Hispanic population."[25] The report cites that "nearly forty percent of Catholics in the United States are Hispanic/Latino/a and ten percent are African American, Asian-American, or Native American. Among millennial Catholics, fifty-two percent are Hispanic/Latino/a."[26]

In the national synthesis for a synodal Church in the United States called by Pope Francis, the synodal consultations identified that more work is necessary to welcome diverse cultural and ethnic communities. For example, one region stated, "Rather than divide us, our diversity should be a source of strength."[27] Many acknowledged the ongoing "need for deeper cultural understanding, more diversity in parish life: in faith formation, liturgical celebrations, and social experiences."[28] This synodal synthesis supports the strength of a multicultural Church and appreciative inquiry as a necessary tool in listening and accompaniment: "There is increased strength to be found in councils, committees, groups, and activities within the Church that are diverse in age, race, and life experience, as a variety of perspectives and understanding can allow for more effective ideas and actions to arise."[29]

Race and ethnicity were not the only spillover. Women lay ecclesial ministers critiqued the organizational culture in the Church. They see themselves as marginalized in decision-making processes.[30] In this instance, gender contributes to disengagement in the workplace. "Women on parish staff said they felt underappreciated, underpaid, not supported in seeking formation, worked long hours, and lacked good role models for self-care."[31] Stories of marginalization continued with other groups such as youth, people who are divorced, and the LGBTQ+ community. One parish community, for instance, begged for guidance: "We believe we are approaching a real crisis in how to minister to the LGBTQ+ community, some of whom are members of our own families. We need help, support, and clarity."[32]

> PAUSE FOR REFLECTION
> - What spillover influences how you see your ministerial work?

Triggers of Identity Conflict

In their stories in chapter 1, our eight writers point to triggers that emerge in everyday ministerial experiences. Understanding and identifying triggers is a foundational skill needed to lead and minister across differences. Triggers or a triggering event can be an action or series of actions that creates a noticeable perception of inequity or inequality related to social identity. They may be rooted in biases. Usually, triggers are emotional in nature as they impact the heart of who we are and what we believe. The chain of events that triggers a reaction involves people with differing social identities, such as a newly hired lay ecclesial minister and one who is seasoned, or a lay ecclesial minister and an ordained priest, all of whom may have different national identities. The ability to minister across differences is essential, yet many people do not know how to do this.

There are five types of events that trigger social identity conflicts in the workplace:

- *Differential Treatment* triggers occur when one group perceives that another group has an advantage when it comes to the allocation of resources, rewards, opportunities, or punishments. Recall Timothy Johnston's experience in which a promised distribution of resources was subverted by favoritism.[33]
- *Assimilation* triggers occur when the majority group expects that others will act just like them; there is an expectation that non-dominant groups will blend into the dominant culture. This is part of the dilemma Dorice Law faced as she entered a chaplaincy staff in which she quickly became marginalized.[34]
- *Insults or Humiliating Acts* triggers occur when a comment or a behavior devalues or offends one group relative to another. When Kyle's need for extra assistance for the Christmas liturgies was dismissed, he found the encounter insulting.[35]
- *Different Values* triggers occur when groups have decidedly different values and a clash of fundamental beliefs regarding what is wrong and what is right. Bob Choiniere described a poignant situation in which values he had about organizational life in the Church were ignored.[36]
- *Simple Contact* triggers occur when anxiety and tension between groups is high in the broader society, so simple contact between these groups triggers a reaction. For Kristi Bivens, while she may have become "used" to people dismissing her sense of vocation, it made her feel trivialized.[37]

Barbara once was working with students who were doing a semester of field education in parishes or other religious institutes. Each would theologically reflect on three critical issues during the semester. One of the typical issues was a conflict. In the reflections students wrote, it was often someone else who was the problem. One story involved a young Roman Catholic monastic seminarian from Vietnam studying in the United States. His conflict was with a woman in his parish. As we (the class) delved into the conflict, his issue was with divorced women generally. He judged all divorced woman as immoral. Barbara and he looked at the data for divorces in the United States. In 1950, 2.8 percent of married couples in the United States divorced;[38] in 2021, the divorce rate of married couples was about 15 percent.[39] The student raised his eyebrows and said that they didn't have divorce in Vietnam. In fact checking data on divorce in Vietnam, they found that in 2013 there were 145,791 cases of divorce. Further demographic data "found that women accounted for 70% of people who forwarded their divorce cases to courts."[40] Initially the trigger for the seminarian was *different values* between women in Vietnam and the United States. Because his connections outside the monastery were limited, the seminarian found the data about divorce in Vietnam eye-opening. He engaged in cultural humility that led him to listen to women who were divorced and hear their stories. He also learned that he had blind spots that could be uncovered by further exploration, listening, and attending to one's curiosity.

PAUSE FOR REFLECTION
- Are there certain triggers associated with painful experiences in your life? If so, what impact might that have on your ability to see other perspectives regarding similar situations?
- How do you try to express your perspective with someone very different from you without trying to convince the person that your way is the right way?
- How comfortable are you listening to a perspective that is very different from your own? How do you tend to react when you feel your values are challenged or threatened?

PAYING ATTENTION TO FAULT LINES

Inevitably, work group members differ on a variety of dimensions such as gender, age, race, nationality, educational background, models of Church, organizational tenure, and vocational status. Fault lines occur when different dimensions of diversity converge, creating subgroups so that the members of one group are less motivated to cooperate with members of the other group because of a lack of trust. Because people prefer to interact with people with whom they have more in common, subgroup formations can lead people to conjure "us-them" distinctions. The use of one's power can negatively increase polarization or positively bridge differences. Misuse of power in a context of differences often results, intentionally or not, in the daily injustices (microinequities) that render some people invisible, disempowered, and unacceptable because of their differences. Consider a statement by a male parish director during a staff meeting: "Oh, Marjorie knows I am just kidding when I say she is primarily guided by emotion." Triggers act as a sign that conflict may bubble to the surface. At some point, for instance, Marjorie may no longer tolerate being trivialized. Some fault lines may open, and other times they may remain dormant. Thus, awareness can channel the use of power to engage a difficult dialogue or shut it down.

> **PAUSE FOR REFLECTION**
> - How motivated are you to interact with diverse others despite challenges or conflict that may occur?
> - How much enjoyment do you get out of working with other who have identities different than yours?
> - What are the barriers, if any, that prohibit you from readily interacting with diverse others? What are ways that you might improve and eliminate any barriers?

Diversity and equity only achieve justice when inclusion happens. Thriving then begins in countless ways. To truly ignite the power to make a difference and minister across differences, one must look inside oneself to uncover blind spots, prejudices, preferences, and biases. To be an inclusive leader, writes Jennifer Brown, "one leads with additional vigilance, care and intention to perceive and then address what might be getting in the way for others around them."[41] In the Church, diversity and inclusion are rising priorities. Diversity without inclusion is not enough. Inclusion is much more than just being "nice" to people or even just being aware of unconscious biases. Inclusion involves both being fully ourselves and allowing others to be fully themselves in the context of engaging in common pursuits. Inclusive leadership is intentional and requires effort. Inclusion of diversity means adaptation and building bridges to differences.

What does inclusion feel like for a person? "She or he feels fully present and involved," writes Ferdman and coauthors, "believes that others recognize and appreciate their contributions, and feels both safe and open about their social identities.... [They experience] being able to bring one's whole self to work and the sense that diversity is recognized, attended to, and honored."[42]

PAUSE FOR REFLECTION
- Think about a specific time when you felt especially included and valued in a diverse organization or team, and others there did, too. You felt effective, valuable, successful, engaged, authentic, complete, proud, and alive at work—you could be fully yourself and contribute fully to your group and Church.
- Share a brief story about that experience. What happened? What was it like? What did you feel?
- Explore what it was that helped you to feel included. What did you do? What did others do? What did the Church and its leaders do?
- What did you learn about inclusion? What are the traits of an inclusive leader? How did it feel to explore inclusion with your co-workers?

MAPPING MINISTERIAL INTERACTIONS

We have been discussing many dimensions of culture and identities, some of which are visible; most are not. Cultural identities are components of self-based or socially constructed categories that teach us a way of being, thinking, and behaving. Social identities are components of self-derived from our involvement in social groups in which we are *interpersonally* invested. Our personal identities are components of self that are primarily *intrapersonal* and connect to our individual interests and life experiences. Some of our identities give us power, others marginalize us.

There is not a one-directional, sequential line that makes ministering across differences predictable. In fact, the process is two-directional: culture not only affects who and how we are, but culture influences what we see and how we see it. Values are formative, and they are deeply embedded in us. This information gives us clues to how people feel about the world, respond to situations, and live their lives.

While no one can predict what another person thinks, will do, or will say, values tell us something about what to expect and give us clues about how to work with people from a cultural background different than our own. It is important to remember that we and our co-workers are individuals who have been influenced by multiple cultures—where we have lived, gender, education and professional training, socioeconomic status, age, sexual orientation, spiritual tradition, and so on. We need to be vigilant not to stereotype each other or box each other into some category. We are all unique, the products of multiple differences and our own personalities growing out of them. Understanding differences is helpful in perceiving a central tendency of a group of people, a culture. To achieve real understanding requires cultural humility as a tool for inquiry, discovery, reflection, and dialogue. Notice that our core values are interconnected; it is important to not view them as separate and distinct concepts but as interrelated components.

As a member of her local diocesan synodal advisory committee, Barbara observed her relationships with the nine-member team. People liked one another and had worked on different committees at other times, and yet they still struggled as they designed and implemented the process they would use. Barbara observed the different identities within the team and mapped them to depict differences at play among members of the team. The following chart depicts the complexity of the group based on their different identities.

TABLE 3.1: MAPPING DIFFERENCES WITHIN A TEAM			
Identity	Factor	Very Little Difference ⟵⟶	Much Difference
Cultural	Race	X	
Cultural	Gender		X

Continued

SUSTAINING A HEALTHY MINISTERIAL WORKPLACE

Cultural or Social	Religion	X		
Cultural	Nationality		X	
Cultural	Language Spoken		X	
Social	Educational Level		X	
Cultural	Age			X
Social	Position/ Vocation			X
Personal	Strength Finders Results			X

In this group, eight of the members were born in the United States, one in Mexico. Hofstede's dimensions of culture might help explain the struggles that arose. This chart summarizes the diverse cultural dimensions for the two nationalities on this team, one raised in Mexico, the others in the United States

Those born in Mexico are typically collectivist and have respect for those who hold more power, such as in a hierarchical structure. Those born in the United States are more individualist and prefer equality among people. These two nationalities have distinct cultural values as noted in the hexagons below.

Figure 3.4: Mapping a Cultural Identity for Mexico and the United States

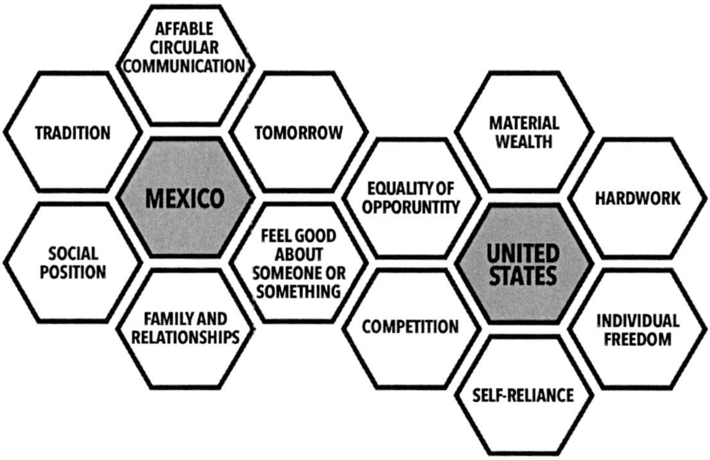

Beyond the Single Story

Another example of how cultural differences can be challenging is based on generational cohort. Yet when a multigenerational team works well together and their strengths are leveraged, they provide innovative perspective and problem-solving skills that advance the mission of the Gospel. The following shows the various generations represented on the synodal planning team and the values they generally carry.

Figure 3.5: Mapping a Cultural Identity for Traditionalists (1915-1945)

Figure 3.6: Mapping a Cultural Identity for Baby Boomers (1946-1964)

Figure 3.7: Mapping a Cultural Identity for Gen X (1965-1980)

Figure 3.8: Mapping a Cultural Identity for Millennials (1981-1996)

Figure 3.9: Mapping a Cultural Identity for Gen Z (1997-2013)

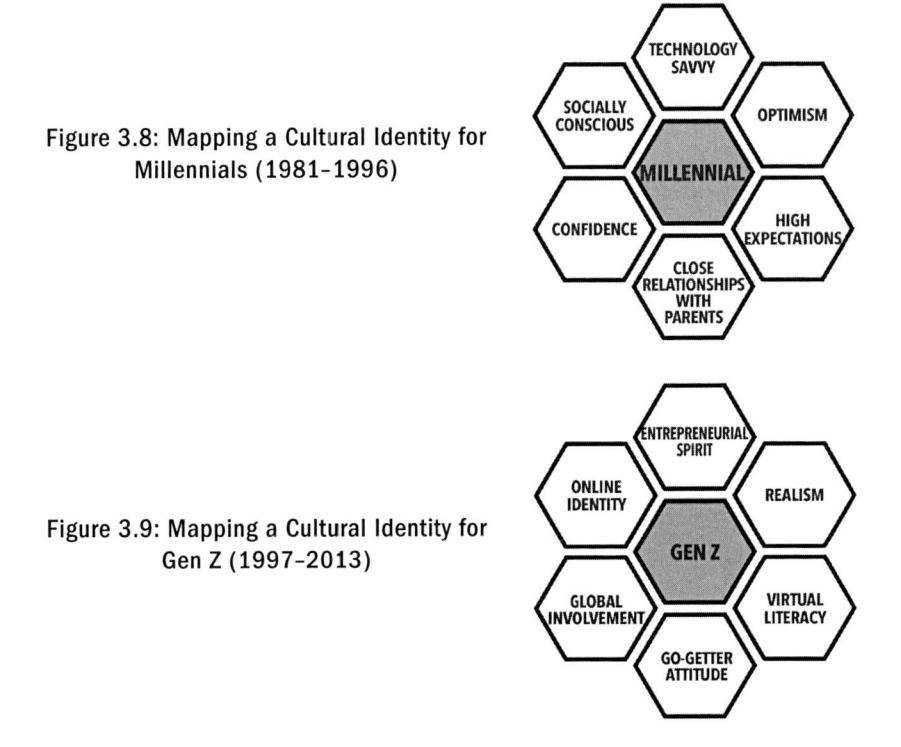

    Another set of differences on the synodal planning team were functional based on positions in a hierarchical culture. Each team member held significant power in their particular workplace. Four people were diocesan staff, two were parish pastoral leaders, and there was a religious sister, retired priest, and pastoral theologian. We all held at least a master's degree. The power in this group was held by two co-chairs, one of whom the bishop appointed; the other (Barbara) was not. They decided on dates for meetings, the agenda, and most other details. They also had different work. Barbara's co-chair described her as "bossy" and, in turn, Barbara described this co-chair as "loosie goosy." The differences in this group became strengths once they were understood. Both had taken the CliftonStrengths Indicator. Barbara's mapping of the results for her and the co-chair proved helpful.

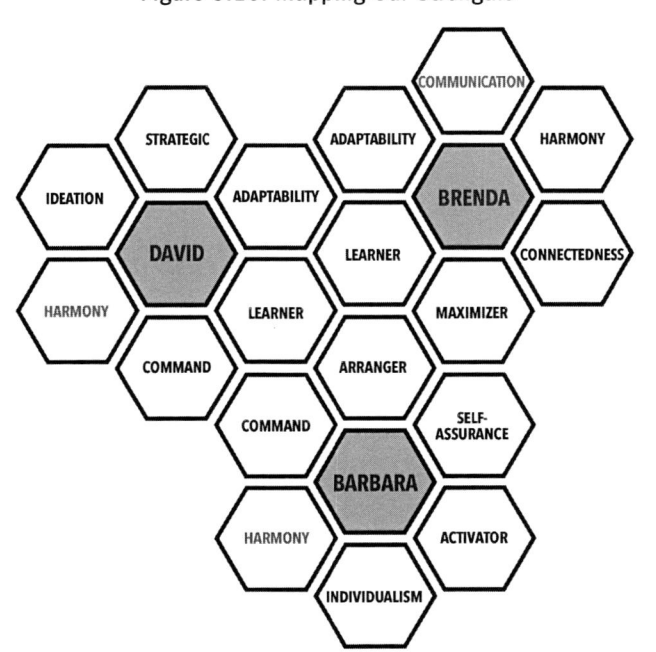

Figure 3.10: Mapping Our Strengths

(Diagram showing a honeycomb of hexagons with names DAVID, BRENDA, BARBARA highlighted, surrounded by strengths: COMMUNICATION, STRATEGIC, ADAPTABILITY, HARMONY, IDEATION, ADAPTABILITY, LEARNER, CONNECTEDNESS, HARMONY, LEARNER, MAXIMIZER, COMMAND, ARRANGER, COMMAND, SELF-ASSURANCE, HARMONY, ACTIVATOR, INDIVIDUALISM)

Certainly, their strengths were different. The real aha moment came when Barbara discovered her own biggest weakness was harmony and the co-chair's was communication. Harmony was the last strength on Barbara's list that she confessed to her colleague. They began to understand their strengths with more empathy. They facilitate many groups together. When tensions rise and need an extra dose of harmony, Barbara steps back, understanding her co-facilitator will be the best person to harmonize the tension. It is a willing surrender of something she thought she needed to control. These strengths are part of our personal identities, components of self that are primarily intrapersonal and connect to our individual interests and life experiences rather than part of the cultural dimensions that define a group. One of the lessons here is that how we interpret a situation is not simply a matter of either national culture or social identity. Interpretation comes at the intersection of many identities.

INEVITABLE DISSONANCE: BUILDING A BRIDGE TO CULTURAL DIFFERENCES

When people of diverse cultures and backgrounds come together in a community there will inevitably be a clash of cultural differences. For example, Fr. Matthew comes from a culture that values following the schedule, timeliness, and completing tasks in an orderly fashion. One of Fr. Matthew's co-workers, Diane, comes from a culture that values spontaneity and has no problem shifting the schedule based on what's happening in the moment. Both Fr. Matthew's and Diane's values are good things. But what happens when you put them together? Imagine some of the challenges they might have working together. Dissonance is bound to happen.

It is important to remember that when we experience cultural dissonance with cultural differences we should not immediately jump to deciding who is right or wrong. In Diane's and Fr. Matthew's example above, both brought a wonderful cultural value to the table. Neither one was "right" or "wrong." We feel it is safe to say that on any given day we can expect dissonance in our ministerial work, whether with co-workers, parishioners, a big new idea, or the daily news. This diagram invites us to approach differences slowly, with an open attitude, rather than closed. It is critical to cultivate an open attitude before dissonance hits. Once it does, it's much harder to go back and adjust.

In figure 3.11, we illustrate the path of a bridge builder who desires to establish cross-cultural relationships. It begins with attitudes. An open attitude assumes the best intentions behind others' behaviors, especially if we might feel unsure or confused in the inevitable dissonance. Acceptance is important. We recognize others for who they are. Being open to another is a willingness to adjust our expectations, our preferred ways of working and communicating, and our comfort zone. Being open to adapt means having the ability to be flexible, especially when a situation, process, or interaction doesn't go the way we planned or hoped.

A closed attitude is the opposite of trust. One is suspicious and assumes the worst intentions. When one is closed, we attempt to justify dissonance in a way that puts the blame on others, thereby absolving ourselves from responsibility. We use excuses to get us off the hook, often creating an "us" and "them" situation. Dissonance can cause us to withdraw physically, socially, or emotionally as we erect walls to stop engaging with a group or culture. Believing that my way or my cultural values are inherently better than others leads to a closed attitude because we see others not as different but simply as wrong.

When we find ourselves triggered, we make a choice to respond or react. We are our better selves when we respond because we listen and place the interests of another ahead of our need to be heard or understood. When we pause, and respond, we recognize our initial assessment of the triggering event is likely not the complete picture. Asking questions is a practical way to humble yourself and demonstrate that you can learn. Dissonance can paralyze us and draw us toward people who agree with us or more like us. When we are in a responsive stance, we initiate good questions, share honestly, and build trust.

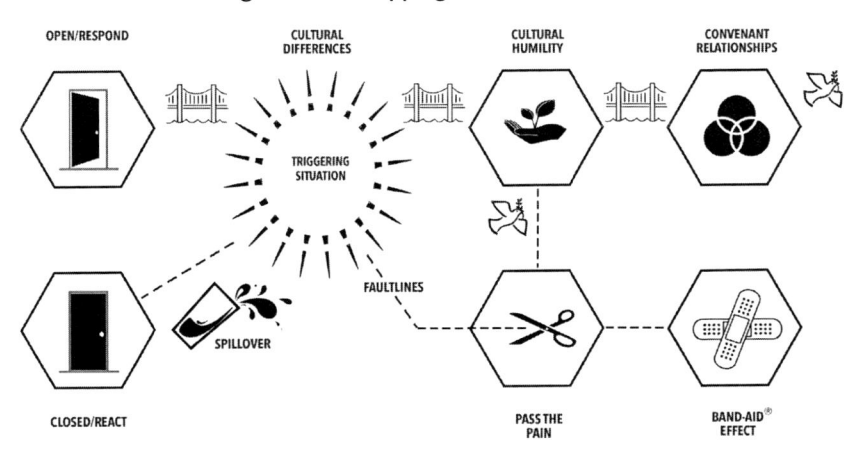

Figure 3.11: Mapping across Differences

From her Benedictine heritage, Joan Chittister writes, "Learning to calm your heart before striking out in emotional darkness is one of the most important dimensions of every response in life. It's the lack of *statio*—of sober consideration of what's happening—that starts road rage. It's the lack of the spirit of *statio* that turns misunderstandings into lifelong enmities. It's the lack of internal quiet and focus that sends you into confusion of thought and chaos of soul."[43] Our spiritual practices matter. Giving our whole self to be present to a triggering event is an exercise in consciousness. It is sometimes a badge of honor to rush from meeting to meeting, or one activity to another, without space for breathing.

"Unfortunately," writes Chittister, "it becomes an excuse to let the hard moments of life go unattended, unthought out."[44]

If one enters a triggering event in a closed-off position, one will experience heightened emotions of frustration and tension, which will lead to a negative response. Eventually, this produces alienation, withdrawal, and broken relationships—and damage to ministerial relationships. Spillover can also raise its head in unexpected ways, and we may be unaware of those parallel triggers as part of the dissonance.

We cannot control the triggering events we experience in cross-cultural interactions, but we can choose how to enter into and respond to that dissonance. When we slow down, we can see the deeper meaning of why there is anxiety. The conscious decision to respond rather than react is a choice we make every day. Such a choice moves unconscious patterns into the light for healing lest we pass the pain along and simply use a band-aid for a quick fix—that is we cover the symptoms, but do not investigate and treat the underlying problem. In other words, we fail to practice cultural humility to know and understand the encounter in order to bring into balance existing power unbalances.

We choose how to enter our day and prepare for the unexpected surprises of human relationships. Once the triggering event is upon us, it is usually too late to pause. To engage cultural differences effectively, we need spiritual practices and self-care to bring our whole person—mind, body, and spirit to our daily work. There are many spiritual practices and self-care tools available to assist us. In recent years, neuroscience is finding that our minds are capable of significant change. Research is finding that "it takes less than two weeks for a neuron to grow new axons and dendrites."[45] Chaplain Bryan Spoon, author of *Neuroscience and the Fruit of the Spirit*, writes,

> For a long time, it was believed that older people could not rewire their brains through new learning. It was believed that habits were more ingrained. Through the work of the fruit of the Spirit in us, our brains have the capacity to rewire even into our advanced years. Secondly, there is Hebb's Law: neurons that fire together wire together. When we practice something, our neural circuitry strengthens in helping us to remember and carry it out in the future. The more our neu-

ral circuits fire together in healthy ways, the stronger these pathways become. The more our will and desires are geared towards love and goodness, the more that our whole person will become an expression of God's goodness.[46]

The work of the Holy Spirit is pictured as a peace dove in figure 3.11. The fruits of the Spirit are love, joy, peace, patience, kindness, goodness, faith, gentleness, and self-control. These spiritual practices produce feelings of connectedness and gratitude. Moreover, as Spoon points out, with these feelings come physiological responses as we experience our breath slowing and muscles relaxing. These responses help us to respond to unexpected triggers. Fear, on the other hand, cause us to react.[47]

Barbara incorporates two practices into her early morning routine: One is a gratitude practice for at least three people: a family member, a friend, and a person she will be meeting that day. She does this before getting out of bed so that checking her cellphone doesn't start her day. Her other practice is to do a body scan, paying attention to lingering stiffness, how her heart feels, and what is on her mind. There is only one intent she seeks: to become more conscious of abiding in God's love and surrendering to it. This contemplative prayer process is not a stress reduction technique; its intention is to be in the presence of the divine. Victor's daily practice varies because he is a poet. He begins by reading poetry and something from spiritual literature that help focus his thoughts. In the meditation that follows, he discovers the first draft of a poem. The process enables him to choose how he will enter the day: responsive or reactive. When he is faithful to his practice, he is less prone to distraction and more aware of how he is present to others. His capacities for kindness and self-control deepen.

Time given over to spiritual practices both benefits the individual and grounds one for engagement in life together. As we will discuss in the next chapter, this sort of grounding is essential for the power of covenant as a framework for the ministerial workplace to merge. Co-workers are more readily able to consent to let the divine act within the group and to create the foundation for meaningful, sustainable change in their work culture.

YOUR LEADERSHIP NETWORK

"We work in silos" is a typical lament of co-workers. This silo mentality represents a reluctance to share information between co-workers or across different departments in the workplace. Having a strong and diverse network exposes one to different perspectives, shared information, and resources. This invitation gives you an opportunity to map your leadership network.

Activity 3: Mapping Your Leadership Network

On a blank piece of paper draw circles representing groups or individuals with whom you regularly interact or depend on to "get things done" at work. These people can be within or external to the organization. Likely categories of people to include are supervisors, peers, direct reports, mentors, and advisors. You may want to include the connections between the different individuals and groups with solid or dotted lines, depending on strength of connection.

PAUSE FOR REFLECTION
- Examine your network and reflect on the following questions. Where do you go to get information? Where do you go to get advice? Where do you go to get support? Whom do you trust? Whom do you think trusts you? Are there certain types of people with whom you have a strong connection? Are there certain types of people not represented or with whom you have a weak connection?
- Apply a social identity lens to your network. Consider to what extent the members of your network "look alike."
- Are members of different social identity groups underrepresented or not represented at all? If yes, which groups are they and what are the potential consequences of not being connected?

Having connections to different social identity groups provides important insights into differences as well as lessons about building relationships and making alliances. Networking is essential to effective leadership. Co-workers who are skilled networkers have access to people, information, and resources to help solve problems and create opportunities. Those who neglect their networks are missing out on a critical component of their role as leaders. While having a diverse network may sound like something that is good to do, if you do not take the time to really think about the benefits of having a strong diverse network or the consequences of not having one, you probably will not be motivated to do much about it.

> PAUSE FOR REFLECTION
> - Consider your experiences with your network, describe the value to you of networking, and identify ways to expand your network.
> - How has networking with different identity groups helped or hurt you professionally?
> - Describe situations in which networking with different identity groups helped you accomplish your work or got in the way of doing work.
> - What opportunities have you potentially missed by not networking with different identity groups?
> - What work-related goals or expectations relate to a need to network with different identity groups?
> - How would you benefit by networking with different identity groups?
> - What steps can you take to build a more diverse network?

These reflections on examining your leadership networks are important. Our leadership networks, our relationships with one another should reflect the doctrine of the Trinity as the model of community in our workplaces. While one cannot overlay the same structure on our networks, the relationships among them can be given the same charge: to "love one another as I love you" (John 15:12). The task of imagining Christian community—or in our case a community of co-workers—was also the work of the earliest Christian community. The triune name is an expression of the intimate union of three persons. It concerns God's life with us—and our life with one another. God is also one because the three persons are in covenant together. Because of their great love for one another, these early followers were of one heart and soul.

The theoretical framework of the doctrine of the Trinity yields a wisdom, a discernment, and a guide for co-workers in the vineyard of the Lord and it is a transformational historical model for the ordering of interpersonal relationships. While the doctrine of the Trinity will not solve all the problems of the workplace, it serves as a critical theological function to critique our life in relation to God.

We know that many aspects of leadership are timeless, such as setting direction, empowerment, and influencing others. It seems imperative from the eight narratives of lay ecclesial ministers that to inhibit triggers from widening fault lines, building confidence and inspiration with our co-workers is necessary. We need to reorient and expand our leadership competencies so that our workplaces are committed, and supportive of diversity, and co-workers feel highly included.

Status and hierarchy effects can cause some co-workers' contributions to be valued and attended to disproportionately. When an ordained person or senior executive is present in a meeting, his or her views are likely to have an undue influence on the outcome. This high power distance often leaves lay ecclesial ministers feeling that they've been placed in an inferior position without access to the decision-making process. In the United States, by most accounts, we reject hierarchical culture and lean toward individualism and equity. For some, the gap is so wide they have little hope for working together. Consequently, we lose the capacity to listen to one another, love one another, and forgive one another. When we hold tight to our identities and personal values, certain that "my" way is God's will for the team, we undermine any potential for teamwork and produce minimal results with little innovation.

Relationships do not happen willy-nilly, without boundaries or accountability. Building better relationships doesn't mean a co-worker needs to become a best friend, but it does require that you get to know them as individuals. As a team member, co-workers create psychological safety and empower charisms and strengths for one another. Here we recognize it is less about what you do, and more about what you enable. And that is a very different skill set. Often, in an individualist culture the natural tendency for team members is "Just give it to me. I can do it better than you can." That does not build a team or a covenant culture because one is focused more on output than creating a covenant culture. Organizational leaders facilitate the entire system, managing change, culture, and strategies. An inclusive leadership model provides for a breadth of possibility for creating a covenant culture in which we commit to one another, as a team, and agree to support one another. Here, inclusion is key. When people feel that they are treated fairly, that their uniqueness is appreciated and they have a sense of belonging, and that they have a voice in decision-making, they will feel included.[48]

In chapter 4 we turn our attention to covenant relationships. In a covenant community we are all accountable for the work we have been called to and to the community we serve. As a good leader, each of us will let a person know when she or he falls short and provide guidance on how to improve. When we engage others to solicit their reflection, feedback, and interpretation of our decisions, we create an environment of humility, empowering the team to help us be more effective in our ministry.

Chapter 4
CALLED TO BE EXTRAORDINARY

As detailed in chapter 3 and illustrated by the stories of ministry that opened this book, working across differences is demanding. It calls for paying attention to the interpersonal dynamics of the group as it forms around a common mission because of the differences each member represents. Each is deeply shaped by their families, the communities in which they were raised and formed in the faith, and by experiences that govern how they interpret the world. People see the world through different lenses, guard their political, cultural, and theological assumptions, and vary in the effectiveness of their skills for contributing to healthy group life. To assume that we can form a work group and naturally know how to navigate such rich and varied differences is naïve at best. At worst, it can make life in the vineyard brittle and harsh.

In this chapter, we explore how to engage the process of becoming extraordinary as a team of co-workers. It involves, as we showed in the previous chapter, understanding the identities we carry. They are important and integral to who we are. At the same time, as disciples of Jesus, we embrace a transformative identity. It is a new identity as preached by the apostle Peter: "But you are a chosen race, a royal priesthood, a holy nation, a people of his own, so that you may announce the praises of him who called you out of darkness into his wonderful light. Once you were 'no people' but now you are God's people; you 'had not received mercy' but now you have received mercy" (1 Pet 2:9–10). In a sense, covenant living as we describe it in this chapter draws its strength from a "new identity" in which we work daily to incorporate the values and principles of covenant into how we interact with others, how we speak, contribute to shared work, and practice living as the body of Christ in all its diversity. This is the lifeblood found in vocational aspirations as described by Frederick Buechner: "The place God calls you to is the place where your deep gladness and the world's deep hunger meet."[1]

Gaining a clearer understanding about ourselves and various identities leads us from "who do you say that I am?" to "who do you say that we are?" The sole purpose of all God's work to conform us to the image of Christ is that we might become what God created us to be in relationship with God and with others. This is why Jesus summarized the whole law as the call to "love the Lord your God with all your heart, and with all your soul, and with all your mind, and with all your strength…[and] love your neighbor as yourself" (Mark 12:30–31).

Each of us has a cultural perspective about the workplace influenced by the hierarchical structures that define the Church as an organization. For some that may make the challenges posed by this chapter seem impossible. Cultivating covenant relationships always seems easy when it involves people we like, people who appreciate us and share our values. The challenge of cultivating covenant rapidly steepens when we lean into the differences among us. Moreover, it is complicated by inadequate leadership, lack of respect, role conflict, work overload, poor communication, a sense of powerlessness, and the absence of psychological safety. As we learned from the study of burnout, ministerial co-workers experience disengagement more than burnout. Further, the behaviors of disengagement Maslach describes are often a consequence of situational circumstances. People on the outskirts of hierarchical structures often feel ignored or disempowered as evidenced in some of the stories in chapter 1. It takes courage and practice to give feedback to those who misuse their power to simply get their own way, control resources, or make decisions inconsistent with the values and vision of the mission of the gospel and stated missions of our institutions.

Because of that seeming impossibility, we argue in this chapter for the empowerment found in covenant-based relationships. Creating a covenant culture requires courage, resilience, and faith, calling forth each person, ordained and lay, to be the best they can be. Covenant holds the possibility for deeper, more authentic, and more effective interactions with all those we work with. Michael West writes, "Here all contributions will feel valued regardless of vocation or profession, 'or place,' in the status hierarchy. Here shared leadership ensures that leadership moves between co-workers (even though there may be a hierarchical leader) dependent on expertise in relations to tasks, rather than hierarchical position."[2]

The practice of cultural humility reminds us we are always in the position of learner as we cultivate interpersonal relationships, especially across differences. Cultural humility does not foster timidity; on the contrary, it encourages cultural sensitivity and respect. This, in turn, means attending to the skills needed to navigate effectively in today's increasingly diverse Church. Shaped by the cultures that define who we are, we carry some values resistant to change. Even the values created in organizational culture that are changeable can become immoveable. Think about new employees, for instance, who quickly experience resistance within themselves as they compare practices and expectations in this new setting that don't align with "how we did it in my previous diocese or parish." Resistance rises as well when a newcomer proposes a different approach to a problem: "That's not the way we do things here!" All of this hinders a sense of belonging, effective community building, and inclusion.

Covenant requires a new sense of agency on the part of all co-workers to work toward a new way of being in relationship that opens the door to mutuality rather than superiority, to supportiveness rather than defensiveness, to trust rather than insecurity. Covenant is both a powerful source of motivation and the sustaining power to change the culture of ministry. Our choice of *covenant* as a key force for change reflects our conviction that without a compelling theological rationale, we will be less motivated to bridge the differences we each embody to achieve a new level of coresponsibility for healthy ministerial workplaces. Theological language alone will not resolve the organizational difficulties co-workers experience. At the same time, the needed action for change requires a way of thinking and speaking powerful enough to keep us at the work of reform when obstacles seem impenetrable and progress only a faint wish. We believe the ancient concept of covenant holds the key to fruitful action.

PAUSE FOR REFLECTION
- When you think of covenant in the workplace, what are your first reactions?

- How does your identity in Christ shape your social identity?

COVENANT AS A SPIRITUAL AND PASTORAL DISCIPLINE

Grounding the organizational dynamics of ministry in covenant is a call to sustained effort—every day. It means learning to nurture mutual trust because, as Sherwood G. Lingenfelter argues in *Leading Cross-Culturally*, the highest priority in ministerial leadership is the formation of a community of trust and then "doing the hard 'bodywork' of creating both community and trust."[3] At a practical level, creating covenant relationships requires psychological safety where all co-workers feel included, cared for, and valued, a strong sense of interpersonal trust, and mutual respect. Trust also enables a team to "feel" their way forward together and motivates compassionate responses to one another. Paying attention to effective interpersonal communication also builds trust. Assuming people "know what I mean" or concluding too quickly, "I know what they mean" requires emotional intelligence as well as cultural humility. Trust is essential for building capacity to deal with the failures of group life, the shortcomings of hierarchical systems, the contradictions that find their way into communities of disciples—all of which are normal consequences of group life—without reverting to old patterns of behavior. We maintain that if there is to be a new story about life in the vineyard of the Lord, it must draw deeply from the wellspring of covenant.

We come to this topic with an expression of covenant created with a group of pastoral ministers from our local diocese that has been expanded during the course of this project. It anchors the reflection guide for a covenant ministry presented later in the chapter:

> *A vocation to pastoral ministry is a call to advance the mission of the gospel, embracing the dignity of every person in their individual uniqueness. The work we share finds expression in various areas of pastoral service and leadership. We seek to deepen our awareness of the riches offered by personal, cultural,*

and theological differences. We measure our success by growth in knowledge of God, coresponsibility for the reign of God, and spirit of hope we cultivate in ourselves and in those to whom we minister. Ours is collaborative work, as ordained and lay ecclesial ministers. We form a community of ministerial leaders bound together by a commitment to Christ, his gospel, and the care of God's people. We will risk being transformed. We recognize that creating a healthy ministerial workplace is a call to use our agency in new ways of being in relationship that open doors to mutuality, support, trust, and justice.

Not everyone with whom we discussed this statement was enthusiastic in their response. Some felt that covenant language can be too squishy, too expansive. They favored ways of framing ministerial work life using contractual language to remove any vagueness. Our approach was not to create an either-or choice between covenant and contract. As Richard Gula has noted, they are conceptual cousins, and each has a role to play in the workplace.[4] A covenant does not have the formality of a legal document and is more of a pledge, a promise to work together across our differences for a common good. To be effective, covenants rely on having trust in the other to keep their word. When disagreements and conflict arise in a covenanted relationship, the primary recourse is commitment to engage in honest, sustained conversation that appeals to shared values, personal commitment, a common vision, and the willingness to build mutually enriched relationships.

It is reasonable to ask, "How do we hold people accountable to covenant?" Surely at times, co-workers experience a sense of powerlessness as they minister in hierarchical structures. When the experience of marginalization arises, it often becomes the dominant story. Gretchen Ki Steidle, social activist and author of *Leading from Within*, however, notes that "there is a power within all of us, and the ways we can use our internal power and the power we have from our various identities can transform inequalities and suffering."[5] In a similar vein, Jennifer Brown, in *How to Be an Inclusive Leader*, urges us to assume responsibility for our roles: "As human beings, we are hardwired to believe that someone else will step in and do the hard work so that we don't have to....In fact, the more people who witness an injustice, the less likely people are to step forward and help. This is called the *diffusion of responsibility*."[6] A robust covenant culture acknowledges and affirms the responsibility each person has for acting on behalf of the common good of the group, the community, and the Church.

PAUSE FOR REFLECTION
- Make a list of the qualities and internal values that give you a sense of power and that you can draw on to help you in your work to minister across differences and sustain a healthy ministerial workplace.

COVENANT ROOTED IN GOD'S INITIATIVE

We learn from our religious forbearers that covenant is primarily an initiative of God's love to which we respond in love. Biblical scholar Arthur Zannoni explains that what the Hebrew Scriptures offer us in its stories of God's covenant with Abraham and Sarah and their descendants is how "endurance, fidelity, care, and testing" shape the dynamic and binding power of covenant.[7] It is far from a casual agreement. Nor does it intend to embody the juridical bonds of contract. A covenant is not forced upon someone or a people. Its power, in part, comes from the fact that the invitation to covenant is just that—an invitation to enter into a new relationship. God did not mandate a covenant, nor did God make it impossible to refuse. What we witness in the Scriptures, however, is that once accepting the invitation to covenant, the people of Israel were expected to be faithful to what the covenant required *as God would be faithful to what was offered*. We take heart that God remained steadfast in the face of the Hebrew people's testing of this bond. It was not a matter of establishing a covenant that flowed flawlessly from that point on. Indeed, stories of backtracking, rebellion, and failure to uphold their part of the covenant are stories of imperfection that resound to the current day.

A covenant will be tested; parties will make mistakes, misunderstand, or follow unfortunate detours. But what sustains people in covenant are not simply its eloquent words and grand vision but the fact that people bind themselves together with deep trust. "I will be your God and you shall be my people" (Jer 7:23) is only aspirational until the testing comes. The commitment to God and one another in covenant is, in a sense, a handing over of our very selves to another (which is why covenant is most often used to describe marriage). When things run smoothly, we never think about not relying on the other. But when crises arise, when disagreements, miscommunication, and seeming betrayals occur, our fidelity to trust calls us to a profound level of re-engagement. As Zannoni reminds us, "Regardless of how many times humans fail to keep the covenant, God never reneges on the promises made, for God is consummately faithful and compassionate to all."[8] While human commitment to a covenanted workplace may not have the same steadiness as God's, staying at the demands of covenant requires more than casual observance.

Walter Brueggemann wrote long ago, "The central affirmations of covenant stand against and subvert the dominant forms, patterns, and presuppositions of our culture and of cultural Christianity."[9] In this dramatic assertion, Brueggemann believes the imaging of a God aloof from the world and its groanings strays gravely from the deeper sense of a bond *between* God and humanity for which "covenant" is the more genuine expression. In that relationship, we see with greater depth, open wide our search for understanding, and practice forgiveness that reforms our hearts and the structures we create. This "subversive character" of covenant finds its way into how Anglican priest Nontombi Naomi Tutu sees the prophet Amos's sense of covenant operative in a Church she visited in South Africa. There, the focus was on embodying the covenant not as a form of denominational identification but as a fundamentally "new way of being in community and to show that worshipping God is about every aspect of their lives."[10]

It is this commanding vision that underlies our use of covenant. The easier part is crafting a statement. Church ministers are good at being able to use theological language to cast a demanding vision. The challenge comes when one must test the conditions of the workplace against that vision—contracts, policies, pay scales, employee handbooks, the conduct of meetings, resolution of conflict, assessment of workload, the quality of our relationships, and even the allocation of resources. It also challenges misuses of personalized power, write Woods and West, as evidenced in "acquiring information that is of value to others and not making it available; building cabals that accumulate power, information, and resources; undermining others' power and success; using aggression and intimidation overtly or subtly; and manipulating uncertainty to difficult situations to accrete power and influence. Such leadership may also focus and sustain, extend, or strengthen hierarchies so that leadership power is protected or enhanced."[11]

Covenant is a way of thinking and acting that centers ministerial practice in theological convictions at the core of vocational call. Ministry flows from and into God's grace and love and enriches the nature of working relationships. Without a doubt, the embrace of covenant is costly. It requires significant shifts in the accustomed patterns of interaction and communication within ministerial teams. It demands time and consistent attention—reciting the covenant pledge is a poor substitute for staying in relationship when matters get difficult, disagreeable, and even hostile. We come freely into covenant, and our agreement to do so must be chosen again and again. We need to examine our structures and processes to ensure that they embody "covenanting." We need, finally, to reconceive leadership in Church organizations so that the aspirations of covenant do not simply overlay on traditional models of leading but compel people to embrace fresh ways of interacting and collaborating that nurture the health of the ministerial workplace.

THE INDISPENSABILITY OF TRUST

Trust is a fragile asset. As noted, a covenant cannot work—will not work—unless those who bind themselves with it commit to actively cultivate a deep sense of trust in each other. This too will take sustained self-awareness and deeper understanding of differences. As much as we might want to assume this is easily achieved for those whose lives are immersed in Christian discipleship, experiences in the vineyard tell us otherwise. That is evident from some of the ministry stories offered in chapter 1.

Trust is perceived differently in dominant and non-dominant groups. Because of their past group and personal experience, "non-dominant group members may have limited trust for those in the dominant group and the systems they have created. This difference in perception and understanding can lead to significant workplace problems because as both trust and respect, independently, decrease, miasma increases."[12] *Miasma* is characterized by an opaque atmosphere of misperception and distortion, where social outsiders (non-dominant co-workers) are subjectively penalized for being different.[13] Trust may be significantly more fragile than those in the dominant group are willing to recognize. In such circumstances, this may make the workplace more strained and difficult to navigate, and the possibility increases for misunderstanding and sundering of the tenuous trust that does exist.[14] Kelly Hannum and her co-workers at the Center for Creative Leadership write that the experience of the nontraditional co-worker is their truth. "For in a state of miasma, perception is reality in very real terms—as when it takes them longer to be promoted than it takes their dominant counterparts or when they must prove and re-prove their qualifications."[15] It should come as no surprise that in such situations people leave their jobs for work in environments more hospitable and open to their differences and the contributions they can make to the work of the organization. Once again, cultural humility becomes an essential tool in counteracting the forces of miasma and strengthening perseverance to establish a covenant culture.

> PAUSE FOR REFLECTION
> - Think of a time when your practice of cultural humility helped build or strengthen relationships in your ministerial practice.

Despite the challenges posed by covenant, Richard Gula would still argue that it is a compelling way to think about the professional character of ministry.[16] Gula grounds his opinion in the idea of vocation that is core to service in any of the ministries of the Church. Everything associated with carrying out that work finds its purpose and energy in what God is calling us to do. In addition, Gula finds a covenant model of ministry more responsive to the fluidity of day-to-day ministry. Ministerial flexibility, for Gula, does not justify inordinate expectations placed on ministers. Here is where the clarity of contractual language helps to address the limitations and boundaries that need constant attention during the whitewater experience of ministerial life. Requests and expectations that lead to overwork and the risk of burnout cannot be justified by appeal to our covenant. While covenant calls for a generosity of time and energy, being clear about how a group pays attention to the needs and limitations of its members is what keeps covenant from being misused. As situations arise in which ministers feel the walls closing in upon them, it is against the spirit of covenant to encourage them to simply stay the course.

Covenant is a demanding, yet compassionate, framework for ministry. Negative reactions to covenant reflect people's experience. The too-frequent lack of specificity of expectations and processes of mutual accountability raise the specter of unfair and unjust treatment. Having a contract with its force of law seems to be a firmer basis for a healthy workplace. Gula respects those who favor contract over covenant but would encourage them to consider three aspects of covenant that keep its biblical roots prominent and active in practice: love, freedom, and trust.

The idea of *love* when speaking of ministerial relationships is not sentimental wistfulness. It is imitative of God's own love as the first move in forming a covenant with humanity. Love as genuine affection for the gifts and attributes of each individual is the dynamic force that sustains a relationship over time and flows from the principle of respect for all persons embedded in Christian tradition and its view of community. Love is not abstract but built on knowledge of the other; knowledge takes time and conversation, a curiosity to understand the world from the perspective of the other. *Freedom* in forming covenants is indispensable. It requires personal agency rather than heavy-handed hierarchical mandates. But once we accept to live in covenant, our free choice means that we will stay faithful to our commitment despite difficulties that will arise along the way.

The mutuality of *trust* is one of the dazzling features of God's covenant with humanity. In a world that can often disappoint us in the actions of our leaders, our communities, and the people we encounter, we believe that God's faithfulness will abide. And we strive to be trustworthy despite our own failings and shortcomings. This notion of trust that is bedrock to God's covenant lays out a path for ministerial workplaces. If we lose trust in one another by our actions, our capacity to work together weakens dramatically. We grow suspicious, second-guess motives, harbor grudges and hurts, and often begin to distance ourselves. Trust is a centripetal force; mistrust is centrifugal. Trust thrives in mutuality among co-workers. It is not the responsibility of those in formal positions of authority but is shared broadly by everyone. It is built day by day through humility, right relationships, mutuality, justice, inclusion, and transparency.

The practices for cultivating trust are neither mysterious nor highly specialized. They reflect what we know about how human relationships work: we tend them, or they wither. There are three key practices that nurture trust.

The first is to *be intentional* about understanding differences. They matter. Differences can lead to misunderstanding and increase complexity and messiness in a staff, the sort that begins the erosion of trust. Being intentional means resisting the too frequent temptation to wait and see how a deteriorating situation will play out. That squanders time. In a covenant mindset, as soon as we recognize that mistrust is rising, we name it and seek to understand its causes. Then we initiate conversations and stick with them during the uncomfortable phase in which everyone feels the centrifugal pull of avoidance. Being intentional reflects the nature of covenant as a mutually made agreement to be in relationship for a common good.

The second practice is to *replace judgment* with *curiosity*. This is especially daunting for established groups in which familiarity convinces members they know each other thoroughly. Being curious becomes critical when working with people with different identities and cultures from one's own. Being curious also avoids a common tendency to assume the motives of others. "Jack has never been in favor of the new approach to religious formation so of course he is going to resist altering the confirmation process." Instead of pigeon-holing Jack, one could be genuinely curious about what Jack is really thinking, feeling, and valuing *in this instance*. When we judge, we stop listening. When that happens, we compromise the covenant we made. The story of covenant recounted in the Scriptures models ongoing learning that refraining from judgment generates. Again and again, we hear people asking what God expects of them as persons and as a community. The posture of wonderment that curiosity engenders makes us seekers, not judgers. It encourages the cultural humility we have been discussing.

Finally, test *assumptions and biases*. Assumptions accept something as true or certain to happen without proof. For example, I assume that my co-workers want to change a longstanding approach to confirmation so proceed with my planning and am surprised when there is push back. Bias is an inclination or prejudice for or against one person or group in a way considered unfair. For example, there is a bias that young people lack proper reverence at Mass. Untested assumptions and biases lead us to categorize and caricature others in ways that cause disunity and builds walls. When you meet someone different than you, be aware of which aspects of your own social identity affect how you read what they say or do.

Because trust is the glue of effective relationships, teams of co-workers need to function in ways that specifically, concretely, and consistently build and sustain trust. Without such efforts, our ability to navigate differences limps along. This is the work of leadership that every co-worker shares, not just those with office or position. This understanding of shared leadership for healthy ministerial workplaces comes from the bonding force of covenant: we are in this together, and together we will work toward our shared mission.

COVENANT AS A LEADERSHIP STYLE

How does good leadership, individually and as a team, impact an organization? Moses Pava in *Leading with Meaning* argues that meaningful and useful answers to questions about leadership are available in traditional religions as well as from social science research.[17] Pava shows how religion can address real world problems by exploring the biblical idea of covenant and Jewish leadership. Pava is on the faculty of Yeshiva University in New York, specializing in leadership and business ethics. He is widely respected for his expertise on how *covenant* can reshape and renew the way leadership functions. Pava's model for leadership flows from the themes of shared community, the interconnection of lives, and mutual moral responsibility. In his writing, five key characteristics of covenant have been particularly relevant for us:[18]

- open-ended with mutual responsibility
- focused on general principles rather than specific details
- long-term in nature
- grounded in respect for human integrity
- committed to the identity, uniqueness, and personhood of participants[19]

Pava's exploration of covenants for organizations has clear applicability in ministry settings. There are, of course, individuals who have formally authorized leadership roles, like pastors and department heads.

Because the renewal of ministry and the creation of healthy workplaces are a shared responsibility, however, what Pava presents as qualities of covenantal leaders applies to each co-worker.

For Pava, covenant leaders are ethical stewards whose duty is to pursue the best interests of all, keep everyone informed of the organization's challenges and progress being made, and engage the gifts of all for the missional well-being of the organization. Such leaders actively seek the viewpoints of others especially regarding mission and vision. They want to know the expectations people have of others and the organization itself. And covenant leadership relies on everyone aligning organizational systems and practices with professed values. Constant learning is integrated into the culture of work in a way that enables people to engage in the governance process. From this foundation, Pava advances five core responsibilities of covenant-based leaders:[20]

1. **Inclusive Service.** Because differences matter, are important to the mission, and the organization, people treat one another as unique individuals worthy of respect and empowered to exercise their gifts to the fullest. They recognize where and when they can step in and use their voice to address inequities and they endeavor to tackle those inequities at their roots.

2. **Model of Values in Action.** Values cannot be self-serving. If they are, motivation drops or is stalled. People thrive in a workplace with a strong sense of purpose. Work aspirations connect people to their workplace, their families, and society at large. Co-workers trust one another to seek and receive feedback when values are out of sync.

3. **Continuous Learning and Teaching.** The ultimate learning and teaching vehicle is conversation, especially when it solves a problem, cross-pollinates ideas, creates serendipitous connections, and challenges someone to see situations from a new angle. Old habits and mindsets shift. Covenantal leaders help create and contribute to ongoing learning, evaluation, and reflection as ever-present sources of knowledge—and expertise.

4. **Committed to Truth.** One outcome of ongoing dialogue is recognition that the conclusions and opinions we form are always subject to testing and change. A commitment to truth means learning together what is actually happening, what the evidence of our experience is

telling us, how our assumptions are put to the test, and what impact our actions have.

5. **Empowering Others.** When people can really make decisions and act without asking permission every time, they own the results and can deliver on commitments. Awareness of the obstacles that get in the way of successfully doing one's work leads to finding ways mutually in which people have the resources to accomplish the goals important to them and the vitality of mission.

These five responsibilities of covenantal leadership echo and are enhanced by other approaches to leadership. Jennifer Brown, for instance, expands qualities noted in Moses Pava's work in her discussion of characteristics she finds in leaders effective at advancing equality, equity, and inclusion. Those leaders understand their identities and when to use their power and voice to tackle inequities at their root. They model the behaviors they expect of others, work consistently for the well-being of all, especially for those left on the margins, and are committed to truth and mutual clarity.[21] In her exploration of lessons about leadership drawn from nondominant culture, Juana Bordas shows how leadership characteristics from other cultures deepen the importance of covenant as used in this book. Three principles emerge from her study.[22]

The first is *Sankofa*, which comes from West Africa and is a mythical bird that looks backward and symbolizes the respect African Americans have for the wisdom of the past. In this book, for instance, we are not "inventing" covenant to reform or renew ministry. We are recognizing how this way of relationship draws life and energy from the action of God and humanity represented in the Judeo-Christian heritage we carry. Second, Bordas's own Latino heritage teaches the critical need to understand the power of collective identity—the movement from an isolating individualism to a collective identity. It is the underlying dynamic in Pava's idea of leaders serving others and the need to keep in focus that we are a "we" as we move forward. A third principle Bordas explores is captured in the phrase *mi casa es su casa*. It conveys a reflexive hospitality that ensures the circle of welcome is always open, ready to include friend and stranger alike. For leaders, this principle underscores the generosity needed to cultivate and maintain a true sense of mutuality.

PAUSE FOR REFLECTION
- Based on what you have read to this point, which aspects of covenant leadership do you identify within yourself?
- Which aspects might challenge you?

New understandings of leadership that Pava, Brown, Bordas, and many others are advancing underscore the dramatic shift in work relationships in ministry that is needed to effect meaningful cultural change. Ministering out of a covenant is more than individuals working diligently on the development of their interpersonal and leadership skills as important as they are. More significantly, it means rethinking the nature of leadership itself, its virtues and values, and how each member of a team shares leadership responsibilities. If a change in culture is to happen, we can no longer rely on one model of leadership that flows downhill from some imagined peak of the dominant culture. Discovering how covenant and leadership come together involves scanning the whole workplace to identify where things are flourishing and where committed attention is needed. Then people can apply their leadership to strengthen what is working and addressing what is not. That is why we developed the Reflective Guide for Covenant-Based Ministry.

ASSESSING THE HEALTH OF MINISTRY WORKPLACES

As the healthy ministerial workplace project unfolded over three years of spirited conversations among co-workers from across the country, it became clear that we needed tools that pastoral leaders themselves could use to become agents of the change they believed was needed in their workplaces. The Healthy Ministerial Workplace Index introduced in chapter 2 is one tool. Another is the Reflective Guide for Covenant-Based Ministry. It emerged as we invited a group of pastoral ministers from our local diocese to reflect on what such a covenant might look like. We presented the results of their work at the beginning of this chapter, and it bears repeating here:

A vocation to pastoral ministry is a call to advance the mission of the gospel, embracing the dignity of every person in their individual uniqueness. The work we share finds expression in various areas of pastoral service and leadership. We seek to deepen our awareness of the riches offered by personal, cultural, and theological differences. We measure our success by growth in knowledge of God, coresponsibility for the reign of God, and the spirit of hope we cultivate in ourselves and in those to whom we minister. Ours is collaborative work, as ordained and lay ecclesial ministers. We form a community of ministerial leaders bound together by a commitment to Christ, his gospel, and the care of God's people. We will risk being transformed. We recognize that creating a healthy ministerial workplace is a call to use our agency in new ways of being in relationship that open doors to mutuality, support, trust, and justice.

The statement highlights several key components we believe inspire creative, positive action for change:

- It is gospel centered and focused on mission.
- It acknowledges the hierarchical structures of the Church and offers shared principles for all in collaborative leadership, ordained and lay ecclesial.
- It measures its achievement in terms of responsibility, workplace culture, dignity of the human person and work, co-worker engagement, and hope.
- It underscores the collaborative nature of all ministries, ordained and lay ecclesial.
- It is communitarian, flowing from commitment to Christ.
- It acknowledges that ministry transforms the minister as much as those served by ministry.
- It affirms that creating and sustaining healthy workplaces is the work of everyone.

Reflection on the covenant statement can be beneficial for individual ministers and for staff groups. They might even reframe it to incorporate characteristics particular to their context. This meditative reflection on the covenant statement reduces the tendency to give lip service to a new vision while essentially continuing old ways of doing things. For the guide, we want to frame practical elements in the workplace grounded in a theological vision. To that end, we convened a team of partners from other national ministry-oriented groups and ministry consultants to design a reflective guide that integrated vision and practical concerns. Our partners included the following:

- Association for Graduate Programs in Ministry
- Diocese of Saint Cloud
- Federation of Pastoral Institutes for Hispanic Ministry
- National Association for Lay Ministry

The resulting guide (see Appendix B for a full usable copy) is intentional in reminding a workplace group that they do not begin an assessment in deficit. Every staff faces challenges, but it is self-defeating to conclude that all is darkness and there is no light. The guide therefore encourages staff to identify strengths already active in their work settings. Change always benefits when we leverage our strengths as we work purposefully to address obstacles, shortcomings, and blind spots that encumber mission and compromise a spirit of covenant.

Creating and sustaining a healthy ministerial workplace, of course, is both a theological and practical task. This covenant aligns core biblical values and the eight workplace elements we used in this project into twelve principles. The biblical values include identity in Christ, presence of the Holy Spirit, love for one another, unity in diversity, mutuality, gracious speech, and restorative mercy. The twelve principles strive to keep in focus that our aspirations to live out of our new identify in Christ need to influence the practical ways we interrelate and do our work. The reflective guide is not a clinical diagnosis but rather seeks to foster deep, honest reflection as groups work to improve the health of their workplaces through an embodied covenant. To use this guide, individuals on a staff first assess and rank each principle based on their perception and experience, citing examples to support their choice of ranking. Individual assessments are then pooled to provide the staff with an overview of the organization's health. The discussion questions provide a structure for the group's discussion of the results and its decisions for action.

Each of the principles touches on an aspect of a healthy ministerial workplaces, weaving together vocational matters with organizational practice. We provide a ten-point rating scale so that people can be as precise as possible about what they are witnessing in their workplace (see table 4.1). We strongly encourage people to name practices already in place that reflect the principle in action as well as naming obstacles that are getting in the way or impeding the work of mission. It is easy to note deficits that weigh on us but overlook the good we are accomplishing.

Principle 1: We share a conviction that the sacraments of initiation form the common basis for our shared participation in the threefold ministry of Christ, who is priest, prophet, and king. We also acknowledge the complementarity of our distinct vocations as ordained and lay ecclesial ministers.

Principle 2: We gather for prayer, community, and learning, knowing that the inspiration of the Scriptures and theological reflection on our ministerial practice ground us in sustaining right relationships and a healthy ministerial workplace.

Principle 3: Our mission and vision provide the values we seek to embody in every aspect of our work and that those shared values are a primary source of mutual good as we evaluate our ministerial leadership.

Principle 4: We strive to deepen the human competencies needed for effective teamwork and ministerial leadership. These include skills for strong interpersonal communication, intercultural competence, decision-making, management of conflict, ways to process difficult issues, and sustained collaboration across designated positions.

Principle 5: We mutually define a manageable workload that provides the opportunity to serve the needs of the community through one's designated ministry as well as one's charisms and deep passions, to pursue career objectives, and to develop professionally.

Principle 6: We have in place a regular system of evaluation that provides insight into our work performance, raising up our accomplishments and finding resources and ways to address areas of needed growth.

Principle 7: To be in right relationship with all employees and volunteers, we practice being open to receiving and giving skilled and compassionate feedback.

Principle 8: We interact out of a shared understanding that the quality and effectiveness of our professional relationships have significant impact on those to whom and with whom we minister.

Principle 9: We contribute to developing and sustaining a healthy workplace by individual and team ongoing education, ministerial formation, and the cultivation of imagination and creativity in whatever forms they might take.

Principle 10: We work at creating inclusive communities in which we cultivate respect for diversity of cultural traditions, languages, theological visions, devotional and spiritual practices.

Principle 11: We provide in a fair and transparent manner for the just and financial well-being of all employees.

Principle 12: We abide in the covenant through the principle of subsidiarity, when those closest to a problem or pastoral concern will be consulted for deeper understanding.

TABLE 4.1—SAMPLE ITEM FROM REFLECTIVE GUIDE										
Principle 1: We share a conviction that the sacraments of initiation form the common basis for our shared participation in the threefold ministry of Christ, who is priest, prophet, and king. We also acknowledge the complementarity of our distinct vocations as ordained and lay ecclesial ministers.										
1	2	3	4	5	6	7	8	9	10	
This describes us most of the time.					**This does not describe us and needs development.**					
How are we incorporating this practice already?										
What seems to get in the way of living out this principle?										

THE PROMISE OF COVENANT AND ITS CHALLENGES

Development of an employee handbook can be significant in efforts to create clear, transparent, and fair practices to guide how we work together. Such a resource alone, however, cannot create or sustain a healthy ministerial workplace. Embracing covenant introduces the attitudinal shift needed to begin a process of transformation that animates the very heart of ministry—its originating call from God. In covenant, we pledge our trust in God and in one another because we are bound together in faith and mission. We develop our capacities for mutuality in the work we do, but also in how we reach decisions, allocate resources, assess use of time, delegate authority, and manage conflict. Covenant does not promise or create heaven on earth, but it puts into motion a new way of being in relationship. Because it reinvigorates a shared sense of leadership and responsibility in every minister no matter their position, covenant makes the work of building and sustaining a healthy workplace "our work," not "their work." Either we are in ministry together in a way that models our deepest values, or we are just doing a job at the same place. The choice is best embodied in a statement often attributed to the poet June Jordan, "We are the ones we have been waiting for."[23]

Every promised way forward carries associated challenges. In a way, those who would view the covenant statement presented here as inarguable but likely ineffective in practical terms are right. A lovely statement about life in the vineyard cannot in itself change how things are done. For that to happen, ministers need to embrace risk. That is very clear in chapter 3 as we face the necessary challenge of working across differences. We all know the patterns of ministry that exist now. Some are more brilliant than others, but we pretty much know the rules of the game. Deciding to reconstitute as a ministry team in covenant means entering unfamiliar territory where triggers and fault lines can lead us into turmoil, even confusion. As we grow in confidence in the trust we are building, there are five disciplines essential for deepening how we make covenant a dynamic force in our workplaces:

- **Speak the truth; hear the truth.** People have a natural preference to work and socialize with others like themselves. Diversity leads to creativity and innovation. Diverse teams hold the possibility for greater truth to be said and heard. We are adept at indirect conversation or at seeming to agree when in fact we are smoldering inside. We sometimes think that holding our tongues is safer than saying what the situation requires. Speaking truth *with love* is how a covenant-based group interrelates. At the same time, we need to do the sort of inner work that enables us to hear when the truth is spoken to us.

- **Keep the vision central.** There is a practicality to the work of ministry that can lull us into routine thinking. More problematic is when the work we do obscures the vision it is designed to serve. Returning frequently to the vision we share as a ministry team and the mission toward which it points cultivates the common ground we share. However, a desire for harmony or conformity in the group may result in an irrational or dysfunctional decision-making outcome. Cohesiveness, or the desire for cohesiveness, in a group may produce a tendency among its members to agree at all costs. On the other hand is the danger of working in isolation where we each reframe the vision in terms suited to our immediate responsibilities. Praying together about our vision, testing our ideas against it, and assessing what we are accomplishing in light of how it advances vision all remind us repeatedly that we are gathered and sent by God.

- **Desacralize organizational structures.** How we are organized in parishes or departments is of course determined by Church law but not in a monolithic way. Too often, individuals assume that a parish or department needs to be structured in one way only or that power always runs downhill, or one area of ministry deserves more attention and resources than another. Structure is inanimate and is justified by its capacity to facilitate achievement of vision-based goals. We all have preferences and biases about how to run things. In a covenant, we challenge ourselves to ensure that structure serves mission, not the other way around.

- **Increase skills for effective interpersonal communication.** This begins with self-awareness, by delving into your world and heightening consciousness of attitudes, thoughts, and feelings that come through dominant belief systems. The goal of communication is to share meaning. Using the practice of cultural humility helps one observe themself while communicating. Are you able to withhold judgment? Become attentive to when you are surprised by someone's differences. We have gained a tremendous amount of insight into the differing patterns of communication and into the ways we can listen and speak with greater clarity. For example, Brenda Allen draws our attention to the phrase, "I didn't mean it." It can imply one wasn't thinking rather than acknowledging the negative impact and facilitating a conversation for understanding. Such skills are essential for speaking and hearing the truth.[24] They are skills, not aspirations or hopes, but concrete, evidence-based ways that reveal how we can live effectively in covenant.

- **Remember the indispensability of prayer and theological reflection.** If indeed ministry is a vocational call and if ministry thrives best in covenanted relationships, then a ministry group must pray together regularly. This is not the cursory prayer we might say at the start of a meeting to get to the real business, but prayer that creates a sacred pause in all the busyness to recenter in the gospel the work, the long conversations, and the struggles to live in covenant. Theological reflection encourages ministers to recognize how ministerial practice is a source of revelation about God working among us, about the alignment of values and activities meant to advance those values, and how we participate in and draw inspiration from a larger tradition of faith and mission. It is important to draw on themes such as power and privilege, voice, dominant and non-dominant culture in our story, and in God's story. Theological reflection is both broadening and deepening. Sometimes it is disruptive and liberating. It brings together the stories we carry with the great Story that inspires all we do.

Covenant requires time and energy, which we tend to believe are in short supply. However, whenever we excuse ourselves from developing our capacities for covenant and conventual leadership because we are so busy, we squander the opportunity to revitalize the vineyard. In our rush to do everything, we miss the graced moment to be people who have seen a great vision, have heard a stirring call, and have chosen to live in a new way. That choice carries risk, pain, disappointment, setbacks, and the need to begin again. But as our storytellers in chapter 1 tell us, in the midst of all the challenges and opportunities, God is at work. In that we can trust.

Chapter 5

CREATING A NEW STORY

In the opening chapter, readers engaged stories by ministers that reflect one of the eight elements important for a healthy ministerial workplace. Each story presents a telling years after without losing touch with the edge it sometimes carried. In the essays that follow, the writers return to the element at the heart of their story and look at it with a new lens. The essays are interpretive. They result from stepping back from the moment and entering into a new conversation with the challenges noted. What emerges is content for a new story in which the normal and sometimes unforeseen disruptions of ministerial life open to new understanding.

    The reflection questions at the end of each essay are for individual or group use and can be a way to affirm in the readers' own lives the importance of always seeking out the new story.

VOCATION: CALLED TO THIS TIME, THIS WORK

Kristi Bivens

In her narrative, Kristi Bivens recounts the frustration she has felt having frequently to defend or explain her vocational call as a lay, single person in service to the Church. She is triggered by definitions of *vocation* that narrow who is called to ministry and leave her feeling insulted and excluded. While this spillover taints her identity, in her reflective essay she regains agency and shows the sources of her confidence that helps her tell a new story for herself—something that can inspire both new and seasoned lay ecclesial ministers. Kristi demonstrates how her sense of vocation transcends the work she does. Most important, she encourages lay ecclesial ministers to claim their call with boldness and conviction.

Google the word *vocation*. The first links are dictionary definitions. Later, the list of links begins to include Christian, mostly Roman Catholic, sites. If one digs deeper, the list is interspersed with links to college career centers. They all seem to include some variation on the idea of vocation as one of two things: an occupation or priesthood and religious life. Both of these ideas seem to involve a call of some kind. Vocation seems so ordered and simple when one looks at it this way. It is what I do or how I live. But is that truly what vocation is?

As I grew up, I felt I had two choices about my vocation: get married or become a nun. Eventually, the idea of vocation in the Church began to entwine with the idea of the single life as a vocation, so I added that to my list of choices. At the time, few diocesan vocation offices would have said that the single life is a vocation because there is no sacrament or commitment connected to it. Without my theological formation, I might have concluded that indeed I had no real vocation in the Catholic Church.

As I look back, I realize that my life would have been very different if I had been able to think about vocation as more than a set of lifestyle choices set out by the Church. Vocation is a constant questioning and discernment of what God is calling us to in our life and in our work. If knowing our own vocation is not set and predetermined, the definition of vocation cannot be narrow. If, as a Church, we must broaden our understanding of vocation, then as one of the Church's lay ministers, I need to broaden my own understanding and vision of vocation as well.

The U.S. bishops, in the conclusion of *Co-workers in the Vineyard of the Lord*, acknowledge the fact that in preparing their pastoral letter, they recognized a need "for a more thorough study of our theology of vocation….What is 'our theology of vocation'?" they wrote. It seems a simple enough question, but the answer is anything but simple.

The columnist David Brooks states in his book, *The Second Mountain: The Quest for a Moral Life*, "The summons to vocation is a very holy thing. It feels mystical, like a call from deep to deep. But then the messy way it happens doesn't feel holy at all; just confusing and screwed up." A vocational journey is messy. Even though we talk about "the call" as something simple, God does not just pick up the phone and tell us what our vocation is. It requires discernment, counsel, relationships, and knowing ourselves well. None of these things are easy.

In *Introducing the Practice of Ministry*, Kathleen Cahalan defines vocation as

> the response to God's call and the Spirit's charisms manifest in adult life commitments in relation to three aspects of the self: (1) how I live, particularly in relationship to permanent post-baptism commitments; (2) what I do, the service I offer to God in and for a community; and (3) who I am, the sense of self as it relates to my personal, historical, cultural, and social contexts. Our baptismal identity and call to be a Christian disciple is lived out in and through the particular callings that constitute our vocation.[1]

How I live, what I do, and who I am. These three statements offer a much deeper and broader sense of vocation than simply as a state of life as the Church often defines it.

Defining how I live has been the hardest part of my vocation. What is my state of life? For much of early adulthood, the pressure to find another to share my life within the sacrament of marriage was huge. People tried to find someone for me, but these encounters never went beyond a first date. The church I served and loved seemed to have most ministries focused on supporting those with spouses and children. There was also society's pressure that I would not be complete until I found another with whom to share my life. Then conversations deepened about the single life as a vocation. That appealed to me. Was this what God was calling me to? What was vocation to the single life? No one seemed to really know. I remember sitting in my grandmother's living room listening to a vocation director say that it was a life called in service to the Church and the world, in contrast to the vocation of marriage being in service to another and a family. That was the closest I ever got to an understanding of where I thought I was being called.

Creating a New Story

As a child born in the 1970s, I was raised in, as David Brooks calls it, "a moral ecology," best summarized by the phrase, "I'm free to be myself." It fostered a culture of "hyperindividualism" and argued that my accomplishments are the most important thing about me, that I can pull myself up by my bootstraps, and that I do not need anyone but me. This led me to question why I would want to get married. I embraced hyperindividualism because I believed that I needed to be the antithesis of a woman as understood within my practice of the faith growing up. I did not need to be anyone's "helpmate." I was not going to be "submissive" to anyone. The treatment of women in the culture also formed my desire to be as good as a man. My state of life as a single woman became a cause to fight for. The single life needed to be seen by the Church as a vocation on equal footing with priesthood, religious life, and marriage. Embracing single life by committing to a life of service to the Church and others was the next step.

I spent eight years in Catholic education as a classroom teacher. Then I served two rural parishes for ten years as a parish administrator. Rarely did I discern my state of life. There was no need. I was busy taking care of everyone else to the point of not caring well for myself. It was something of a messiah complex. Becoming associate director of lay leadership formation at the diocesan level raised vocational discernment to new prominence. Right now, my state of life is single. Cahalan says that "out of a true solitude and aloneness, the single person lives fully into relationships of mutual love and concern for others."[2]

The second tenet of vocation, what I am called to do, has been the easiest discernment for me. I am a teacher and a formator. I love to learn, and I love the processes that help another to learn. My journey of service began as a teenager in volunteering to teach Sunday School. I have been an elementary school teacher, led Bible studies with adults, and walked with those who have an interest becoming Catholic. Nothing gives me more joy than seeing another understand a new concept and deepen their understanding of the Christian faith. Right now, I have the most life-giving job of my life in service of lay ecclesial ministry. Coordinating opportunities for ministers to grow in faith and ministry is not easy work, but it is good work. It is work needed in the Church and to bring forth the reign of God on earth.

Cahalan's third tenet, who I am, is multifaceted. I am so many things: a woman, a daughter, a sister, an aunt. I come from a predominantly German background, with a little English, Irish, and Scottish thrown into the mix. I was raised in a small town on the prairies of Minnesota where, in the early years of my life, we spent Sunday mornings on the golf course. As I grew up, I became the daughter of a permanent deacon, and Church was the focal point of the rest of my upbringing. All of these things form my identity in this time and this place.

How I live, what I do, and who I am all inform my ministry as a lay ecclesial minister. What does that mean for the broader Church's understanding of vocation? It is not as simple and set as some suggest by claiming a particular role: I am a priest. I am a monk. I am a religious sister. I am married. I am single. Imagine if Jesus had simply come and said, "I am the Messiah?" Would people have understood? In John's Gospel alone, there are seven "I am" statements that he used to help people understand who the Messiah was for his followers: I am the bread of life; I am the light of the world; I am the gate; I am the Good Shepherd; I am the resurrection and the life; I am the way, the truth, and the life; I am the vine. Each of these statements reveals more about Jesus than simply that he is the Messiah. For instance, as the bread of life, he nourishes us. As the light of the world, he helps us to see in the darkness of life. As the gate, he helps guide us to the right places.

What are the "I am statements" that can help to understand vocation for lay ministers? In our common baptism, we are baptized priest, prophet, and king and called to be disciples of Christ. For Cahalan, the basis of ministry is found in discipleship. In light of that, her work grounds "I am statements" for the vocation of ministry: I am a teacher. I am a presider. I am a witness. I am a companion on the journey. I am a prophetic neighbor. I am an administrator.

I am a teacher. The vocation of lay ministry primarily is one of guiding other disciples in understanding what discipleship is. It requires the minister to evangelize and catechize believers and seekers in what it means to be a follower of Jesus through the lens of one who is a follower.

I am a presider. While lay ministers do not preside at the Eucharist, there are many other places in the Church where they lead the community in worship—in prayer services, Sunday celebrations in the absence of a priest, wakes and burials, and devotions practices of the Church. They also set an example for other worshippers by the centrality of worship in their lives.

I am a witness. All disciples of Jesus are called to share their story with others to bring others to Jesus. This most often occurs through one-on-one conversations, but for the minister it can come through preaching. Breaking open the word of God through personal experiences of God can help others see the workings of God in their own lives.

I am a companion on the journey. Lay ministers walk with others. Being with another in times of pain and testing as well as times of joy is a sacred place. It is within this sacred place others can experience the love and forgiveness that can come through Jesus.

I am a prophetic neighbor. As all are called to witness to Christ's love, all are called to speak Christ's words of love, peace, and justice. Matthew 25:31–46 makes it clear that we will be judged on our actions. We have a responsibility to give food to the hungry, drink to the thirsty, clothe the naked, welcome the stranger, care for the sick, and visit the imprisoned. Lay ministers need to lead the effort to respond to the cry of those on the margins of society. They can be the voice crying out in the wilderness for those who are voiceless.

I am an administrator. When God created the world, humankind was given dominion over it. We are responsible for the care of creation and all the goods it offers. An essential part of lay ministry is to steward the gifts of one's particular community as well as the goods and gifts of the world. This is not just about the financial gifts, but the gifts that each person brings to the world. Lay minsters call forth the gifts of others to help serve the world. They promote care for creation and good use of human, natural, and financial resources.

All the "I am" statements deepen an understanding of what lay ecclesial ministry is and what it entails. It broadens the work as more than being "Father's assistant." Authority for lay ecclesial ministry is found in baptism and discipleship.

Let us return to Cahalan's three tenets of vocation and look at them through the lens of lay ecclesial ministry and the "I am" statements. The "how I live" tenet declares that many laymen and laywomen live a life devoted to ministry in the Church. They are living in commitment to something bigger than themselves. It is a sacrificial way of life. The "what I do" tenet affirms that many laymen and -women are paid to do the work of ministry for a living, but because it is also how they live their lives, it is more than a job. The "who I am" tenet manifests that I am a lay ecclesial minister. It is such a simple statement, but so difficult to say in a Church that can seem reluctant to see it as a vocation. Part of the needed change requires lay ecclesial ministers to claim it often and aloud: I am a lay ecclesial minister who has been called to the work of the Church by a God who loves me deeply and wants me to share that love with others.

Vocation is not easy or simple and neither is lay ecclesial ministry. The vocation of lay ecclesial ministry will require constant reflection and discernment. Broadening the understanding of vocation as more than a state of life will help. Cahalan's tenets and the "I am" statements help reveal over and over that the work that begins in discipleship and blossoms into ministry is truly vocation. It is how we live, what we do, and who we are.

COMMUNITY: CREATING SPACE FOR GOSPEL VALUES TO THRIVE

Dorice Law

Dorice Law recounted in her narrative what happened when her sense of community so central to her understanding as a disciple of Jesus and a minister of the Church butted up against the forces of power and lack of cultural humility that can infect both community and ministry. Here she reflects on expectations she had for working on a ministerial team. They were formed in her childhood and confirmed in her ministry formation—that we could be of one heart and mind, united in Christ. This is certainly the vision of people governed by a trinitarian vision of community life. What she found were fault lines related to race, resistance to change, and unspoken understanding of power. Dorice reminds us that becoming the community we seek to be is an intentional act, one that requires not just acknowledging the differences among us but finding the sustaining motivation to keep at the work of building up. Take notice of how her reflections echo many of the principles and practices inherent in a covenant-based ministry.

When I began my formation for lay ecclesial ministry at Saint John's School of Theology and Seminary, I had a notion of community drawn from childhood experiences. I spent my first eight years of schooling at St. Matthew's, a largely diverse Catholic school on Chicago's West Side. It was there I learned that I was "colored." I took notice of the differences: skin color, hair texture, eye shape, and dialect of my peers. But we were all Catholic, so we were all the same in the eyes of the Church. We prayed together, and every Sunday at Church, we were transformed into a community. I belonged! I felt loved and accepted. This was my Christian community, and we were family. We marched along like the ideal community depicted in Acts 2:42–46, encouraged to see our commonality and believe that we could be of one heart and mind, united in Christ.

Through the rich Benedictine identity of Saint John's, I deepened my understanding of the sacred value of community where social awareness of others and creation are essential. I understood Christian community as being a safe and hospitable home for all, a place to discover our uniqueness, gifts and talents, and a place to be of service to the body of Christ. As ministers of Christ, our responsibility is to create communities where gospel values thrive, such as "respect for persons, justice, integrity, an environment in which (all people) are treated fairly."[3] All of the baptized are called to work toward the transformation of their family, community, and Church.

My calling is ministering through chaplaincy and pastoral care. I began my first working experience as chaplain with the same enthusiasm as the newly baptized, expecting a welcoming spirit in a community of co-workers and believing that my uniqueness, gifts, and talents would be valued as an opportunity to strengthen our community. That turned out to be naïve. What I encountered was resistance, and my differences as a person disturbed my supervisor's vision of what a minister looked like. She functioned like a brain, priding herself on rules of etiquette, religious practice, seasonal liturgical colors, and appropriate music and decor. I functioned more as the heart and focused on relationships, remembering personal details about each resident, remembering always to smile, and being mindful of my responsibility to bring comfort and peace. My supervisor and I should have been a great team! Instead, she perceived me as an adversary. I have come to realize that not all ministers desire to promote growth within the body nor will they take the opportunity to discover how the gifts and talents of another can be transformative for the community. Paul writes that just as our human body has many parts and is still one body, so it is for the body of Christ (1 Cor 12:12–26). It too is made up of many parts, each part intended to function differently; yet, still, it is one body!

Evidence supports the assertion that people thrive in communities where there are positive connections between co-workers, characterized by support, collaboration, and positive feelings.[4] Preaching to the community at Ephesus, Paul urged members to "live in a manner worthy of the call you have received, with all humility and gentleness, with patience, bearing with one another through love, striving to preserve the unity of the spirit through the bond of peace" (Eph 4:1–3). Clearly, it is God's intention that we should live in community.

Without a sense of belonging, I found ministry becoming lonely with disappointing rules and regulations that eroded the spirit of community. I was becoming disengaged in my work. The more I was "put in my place," the greater my sense of isolation. I lost a sense of interpersonal competence. I lost my freedom and ability to make choices and build together a network of spiritual care. I know that I am not alone in this experience. Empirical studies have demonstrated that concerns for others and high-quality interpersonal work relationships are critical for job satisfaction and for leading others to work together to accomplish goals.[5] Further research indicates that 50 percent of clergy have thought of leaving the ministry, and 70 percent report decreased self-esteem since beginning ministry.[6]

Harmony and efficiency are the fabric of St. Benedict's community, and his *Rule* is filled with practical tips on how to live a personal life that is holy and healthy. It contains values of organization, accountability, care for people, respect for the emotional fabric of the community, intensity of focus and purpose, and the importance of healthy interpersonal and community relationships. Rank was renounced. Every individual participated in the functioning of the whole community, and none were to be reduced to a mere "human resource."

I was conflicted at times because Morgan had longevity in her work. I wanted to respect her and the hierarchical structure she demanded. Even a Benedictine community is hierarchical. Benedict's vision for community, however, is structured on an egalitarian footing; that is, one's rank, no matter what one's previous background, is determined by the date of entry. In the process of decision-making, each professed member has an equal vote. Benedict builds community before structure.[7] This is instructional for a community of co-workers in the vineyard of the Lord.

An employee mentality often honors structure first and then community building, as if it were just another bullet point in a job description. Jealousy, conflict, and interpersonal feelings disrupt community. Too often, co-workers in the vineyard of the Lord are individuals first and often reject what differs from their ideas of what ministry should look like based on their background, experience, unexamined assumptions and biases, theological and pastoral frameworks, and a failure to understand community as a testimony to God's life in us. How can we expect to be a fruitful vineyard when branches are being torn away and vines tangled? St. John Paul II spoke about the vineyard and the connection between communion and mission in his *Apostolic Exhortation to the Church in Asia*: "Communion with Jesus, which gives rise to the communion of Christians among themselves, is the indispensable condition for bearing fruit; and communion with others, which is the gift of Christ and his Spirit, is the most magnificent fruit that the branches can give. In this sense, communion and mission are inseparably connected."[8]

The doctrine of the Trinity is *not* teaching about God; rather, the doctrine specifies the conditions and criteria under which we may speak of God. Catherine Mowry LaCugna writes, "Entering into the life of God means entering into the life of Jesus Christ, into the life of the Spirit, into the life of others....Living trinitarian faith means living as Jesus lived, in persona Christi: preaching the Gospel, relying totally on God; offering healing and reconciliation; rejecting laws, customs, conventions that place persons beneath rules; resisting temptation; praying constantly; eating with modern-day lepers and outcasts; embracing the enemy and the sinner; dying for the sake of the Gospel if it is God's will."[9]

To the extent that the interactions, pastoral practices, and lives of co-workers in the vineyard of the Lord give witness to the trinitarian life, we will find a sense of responsibility to go beyond self-focused benefits to advance the well-being of the entire community. For that to happen, co-workers must cultivate the willingness and courage to transform community life from within, becoming a learning and praying community with its central point of departure as the mission of the Church to proclaim the reign of God in this time and place. A life of fidelity to the gospel cannot be sustained alone. "The deadliest enemy of community life," writes Kardong, is "to be focused on personal wants and projects… [and to be] correspondingly closed to the views of others."[10] No one is less worthy, less loved, or any less a child of God. We are all called for a unique purpose, and each of us has unique gifts to bring to the vineyard.

VALUES: A SHARED FAITH, A COMMON MISSION

Robert Choiniere

Bob Choiniere illustrated in his narrative the shadow side of what happens when a commitment to live expressed values fails. In his essay, he shows why such failure is so disorienting when it happens by illuminating the way our values as disciples and as a Church provide an evangelizing vision that gives ministry its rightful bearing.

The Church is entrusted to demonstrate the ways of God in the midst of the human community.[11] The presence of the Church in the world is sacramental—a concrete, outward sign and symbol of the deeper reality of the incarnational God. This presence is made known through an articulation of values that flows from the teachings and life of Jesus Christ as found in the gospel and the living tradition. However, the articulation of Christian values alone is not sufficient. Actions and practices based upon these articulated values are the true fruit of the Church's holiness and the foundation of her credibility.

As a child, I was initiated into a Church presented as a beacon of values. My parents, family, pastor, and the religious sisters, who were my teachers, demonstrated a Church that cared deeply for each individual. I came to trust that God loved me because the people who represented God valued me. These initial tender experiences of a caring community remain in my heart as concrete examples of the love of God communicated through the most influential mentors in my life. Those experiences are touchstones of authentic community that would lead me to live out these same values in service to others. During my formative years, I trusted in the congruence between the values that the Church espoused and the ways that Church leaders and members operated. When blatant incongruences sabotaged me later in my ministerial career, they threatened to shake, and even break completely, my own tender ideals.

When actions or practices taken by Church leaders are contrary to gospel values or directly contradict their own teachings, those actions compromise the effectiveness of the Church, damage people, and undermine the presence of Christ in the world. Congruence between values and actions are critical not only for institutional integrity but for safeguarding the ideals of compassionate community that the Church seeks to convey to its people and to the wider world. Therefore, for the sake of integrity, Church leaders must ensure that actions and decisions within faith communities and in ministerial work settings align with professed Christian values.

Christian values find their focus in the practice of right relationship among disciples and towards all others. St. Paul offers abundant teachings for Church leaders and disciples on the values of Christian community life, a concept he called *koinonia*. While always aspirational, his vision has become an articulation of Christian values. "I tell everyone among you not to think of himself more highly than one ought to think, but to think soberly, each according to the measure of faith God has apportioned….Let love be sincere; hate what is evil, hold on to what is good; love one another with mutual affection; anticipate one another in showing honor" (Rom 12:3, 9–10). Paul's articulation of seminal Christian values focuses on the nature of the relationships between and among members of the Church, making the quality of relationships the calling card of the Christian community.

When I consider my own call to lay ecclesial ministry, my first thought goes to the men and women who nurtured and supported me, who believed in me and encouraged me to offer my gifts to the Church. I trusted the Church because I trusted them. I believed in this vision of St. Paul because I witnessed members of the Church who strove to live these kinds of relationships and who showed me that more important than the issue of the day was the way that we treated and regarded one another in all choices and decisions. My choice to offer my gifts as a professional lay minister was an easy one because I had experienced *koinonia* and believed that I would continue to be supported and become an agent of these same values.

In their role as articulators of Christian values, the U.S. bishops have translated these values of right relationship into the modern ecclesial workplace: "All lay Church employees and volunteers function in a workplace that shares both the characteristics of a faith community of co-workers, as described by St. Paul, and the characteristics of a modern organization."[12] For me, this is one of the most attractive aspects of ecclesial ministry. Professional ministry offers the integration of faith and work through mutual nurture. The bond between my co-workers and me rests on a shared faith and a common mission that we could celebrate and rely on. Going further still, the bishops draw the connections between Christian values and personnel practices. "Best organizational practices are consistent with Gospel values. They imply respect for persons, justice, integrity, and an environment in which committed and skilled workers are treated fairly."[13] The bishops even prescribe a method for addressing work-related concerns consistent with gospel values: "Documentation of honest and constructive feedback about deficiencies and subsequent steps for improvement are important, as both formal and informal recognition of generous, Christ-centered and effective service."[14]

These values of healthy working relationships stand in contrast to ulterior motivations often found in the workplace. Business relationships are often transactional where people are only valued for what another can get from them. Secular, religious, and public institutions struggle internally with unjust power differentials, lack of mutual respect, political backbiting, callousness, and interpersonal hostilities. Even social relationships fray as polarization drives a wedge between people. Intolerance, prejudice, and abuse fill the news. In the midst of this, the Christian community is meant to be a countercultural example of a different way of relating what is rooted in the vision of right relationship, mutuality, dignity, and respect.

The tender ideal of a value-laden community of faith is not a childish, romantic illusion. The experiences I had through my childhood and formative years were concrete examples of values in action. They were not a poetic vision of innocence, or a myth made to be broken when the brutality of the adult world inevitably shatters them. Value-based relationships and environments are sustained by deliberate choices of leaders to place these values above all other motives and live them into reality.

Gospel values come alive not simply through words, but through the actual living out of these values among Christian disciples. Gospel values are meant to be practiced in local faith communities and in the modern ministerial workplace. Moreover, right relationship has consistently proven to be the most effective way to spread Christianity. Christians' radical respect and love attract members and are the most powerful force for evangelization. The story of the nascent Christian community demonstrates the power of the community living out their values. "Every day they devoted themselves to meeting together in the temple area and to breaking bread in their homes. They ate their meals

Creating a New Story

with exultation and sincerity of heart, praising God and enjoying favor with all the people. And every day the Lord added to their number those who were being saved" (Acts 2:46–47). In 250 CE, Tertullian echoed the cause of the Church's attractiveness: "See, how they love one another!"[15] Even Jesus pointed to the primacy of loving relationship as the indicator of true discipleship: "This is how all will know that you are my disciples, if you have love for one another" (John 13:35).

Lay and ordained people who enter ministry trust that the practices of the institution will align with the values of the gospel. The bishops themselves confirm this correlation: "Ministry is profoundly relational. This is so because ministry has its source in the triune God and because it takes shape within the Church understood as communion."[16] The way the Church operates and how relationships are lived out are deliberate and intentional because the Church is called to be a living witness of the God of communion.

Publishing perfect value statements is not sufficient. The responsibility of leadership is to ensure that all decision-making and practices flow from these articulated values. The sacred duty of all pastors is to foster an ecclesial environment that is a living reflection of the values of Jesus. If there is no accountability to gospel values, then a disconnected shadow operation can quickly emerge where alternative values operate beneath a projected veneer of authenticity. These dynamics damage the integrity of all involved and degrade the entire institution while creating confusion, malaise, and more.

As my experience in the diocese changed, unspoken and contrary values began to take hold. I noticed within myself and others a deep sadness that also moved through anger, disappointment, and cynicism. Cynicism is a corrosive and insidious cancer that is the result of a deep break between values and practices. In its grip, trust, respect, openness, solicitude, generosity, and zeal all flounder and the tender ideals once planted so deeply become brittle.

Disparity between articulated Christian values and unspoken operational values becomes a scandal, literally a stumbling block on the road of discipleship. The incongruence between stated values and demonstrable action causes people to lose faith in the gospel and the Church. Church leaders who perpetuate injustice and incongruence may believe their actions do not do real harm since they remain hidden and secret, covered by pious talk. However, such actions erode the vital cord that tethers the Church to the holiness of Christ.

Throughout the Gospel, Jesus saves his sternest condemnation for false prophets and hypocrites who outwardly proclaim one set of values but whose actions, often done in the "dark," reveal their true operational values (Luke 11:35; 12:3; Eph 5:11). Jesus warns his disciples to be on the lookout for these leaders and to not be swayed by them. He calls them ravenous wolves in sheep's clothing, snakes and a brood of vipers, whitewashed tombs beautiful outwardly, but full of pestilence within (Matt 7:15; 23:33, 27). Jesus highlights the tendency to outwardly proclaim one set of values but to act out of another set of unarticulated values. These warnings are salient to all religious communities as incongruence between proclaimed integrity and lived values cripples credibility. Within our savvy consumeristic culture, people are adept at identifying hypocrisy. Those who preach one thing but act in a very different manner are called out and dismissed. Regardless of pious mission statements or rhetorical flourishes about Christian values, consumers know instinctively what Jesus taught, "By their fruits you will know them" (Matt 7:16).

Without courage and accountability, values and action can often decouple. The result is a bankrupt charade of eloquent statements about values that butt against incongruent actions. This is what Christ warned against. Christian values can only be effective if Christian leaders and disciples hold themselves and one another accountable. This does not happen by accident or without intention. The real possibility for corruption of values is as real now as it was in Jesus's time. For the Church to remain a credible and sacramental sign of Christ in the world, all Christian leaders must ensure that the values of right relationship, integrity, and justice are operative in all decisions and actions. Good fruit will grow, and then others will see how we love one another. Christ will be known through us.

CONTROL: KNOWING WHEN EVERYTHING IS NOT A PRIORITY

Bridget Klawitter

We all have experience with starting a new position and facing into the possibility of everything that needs doing—

now! Bridget Klawitter came to this position seasoned with experience. In her narrative she walks us through the mindset that shaped her first days. While she had the blessings of her pastor, her own sense of agency provided the discipline and flexibility necessary for her ministry. Balance is important for Bridget and is manifested by having more lifelines than deadlines.

Work is a good thing for people because through our work, we achieve fulfillment as a human being and indeed, in a sense, become "more a human being."[17] This sense of the purpose of work is very significant as we consider the issue of control. Lack of control over work expectations can be a contributing factor to burnout. For this essay, "control" means the opportunity to make choices and decisions, to solve problems and to fulfill job responsibilities.[18] This is in sharp contrast to workplace disengagement experienced as conditions that are often beyond one's control. It is not unusual to hear pastoral ministers lament that they move from one event to another. Matt Bloom describes this in *Flourishing in Ministry*. "Parishioners want their emails and telephone calls answered quickly. We resist giving out our cellphone to avoid a barrage of texts. Mistakes in prioritizing can lead to misallocation of personal and other ministry resources and leave important things undone or done poorly. Consequently, most or all activities and tasks are treated as high priority, and therefore pastoral leaders may feel compelled to make time for everything."[19]

In the Catholic Church, while the overall number of priests is declining, the number of those in lay ministry is on the rise.[20] This includes the 39,351 lay ecclesial ministers who serve throughout the United States as well as those serving in such settings as hospitals, campuses, and prisons.[21] The interpersonally demanding expectations of ministry are ripe for experiencing symptoms of burnout. Adding to this situation are some ministry environments in which lay ministers feel they have no control over work processes, feel powerless, work in isolation, lack a sense of purpose, and have minimal social interaction with co-workers.

My twenty years in professional healthcare administration taught me how draining caregiving work can be—and all ministry draws deeply on our capacity to provide care. Intensive training in healthcare as a ministry of Jesus from the Wheaton Franciscan Sisters helped me identify the gifts and charisms I bring to advancing the reign of God. This proved invaluable as I tackled the lengthy "to do" list in my new position described in chapter 1. I had to wonder if it was humanly possible to accomplish everything and still maintain a balance between my work and personal life. I recalled Pope Francis's message on the Solemnity of Mary in 2016, reflecting that "each full and unreserved 'yes' we say to God is the beginning of a new story." I had said my yes to this position, and so now it was time to start a new journey with a new community, fully embracing the opportunities ahead while taking steps to prevent emotional exhaustion, depersonalization, and reduced sense of personal accomplishment.[22]

Locus of control is a concept that offers a way to consider how we achieve balance and manageability in our work. Simply put, locus of control describes the extent to which an individual believes they have control over the events that influence their lives. According to Zimbardo, "A locus of control orientation is a belief about whether the outcomes of our actions are contingent on what we do (internal control orientation) or on events outside our personal control (external control orientation)."[23] With internal control, one believes that future outcomes reside primarily within oneself while external control refers to the expectation that control lies outside of oneself—the people in charge, those with more power, even happenstance. Significant research exists on the impact of one's locus of control tendencies on life experiences and job satisfaction.[24]

It is important at the outset to recognize that locus of control is a continuum. Each of us has a dominance of either internal or external locus of control. In my case, I have a predominantly moderate internal locus of control orientation and am more likely to see my future as being in my own hands. When I began my new parish position, then, I felt drawn to activities that would improve my situation: working to develop my knowledge, skills, and abilities and gaining insight about the parish from my new colleagues. These activities would enable me to create positive outcomes. Having a moderate, rather than strong, internal locus of control made me better able to accept situations that I could not influence and manage collectivism. As an opposite to individualism, collectivism pertains to societies in which people from birth onward are integrated into strong and cohesive in-groups that, throughout people's lifetimes, continue to protect them in exchange for unquestioning loyalty.[25]

Creating a New Story

Locus of control finds its grounding in Christ. Undoubtedly, there are important strategic questions we need when considering our ministerial work: What is truly expected of me? What is the mission of the parish? Where do I fit into this mission? What are the expectations of the parishioners of my role? At the same time, those questions need to be seen in light of one's ministerial calling: How will my efforts help bring people closer to Christ? How will my choices deepen my own sense of discipleship? How will achieving a measure of control over my work help advance the mission of the Gospel? As *Co-workers in the Vineyard of the Lord* points out, "All of the baptized are called to work toward the transformation of the world."[26] Only in Christ do we understand who we are, how gifts and skills serve mission, and how to discern expectations specific to our ministerial setting.

The culture of an organization obviously has an impact on one's sense of control. Understanding that culture is important in gaining perspective. A ministry setting in which subsidiarity is operative enables those with an internal sense of control to feel empowered to take positive, effective action—to create a positive future. Ministry settings that are more rigidly hierarchical in attitude or in which micromanagement is normative feed into fears and apprehensions with a more external locus of control. The result is feeling a lack of control, sometimes equated with lack of autonomy. This is illustrated by being told what, when, and where to do one's job. Having no direct input on policy decisions affecting one's job, being given more responsibility than can be realistically handled, and/or experiencing no respite as expectations rise all contribute to excess stress and are overwhelming. A 1986 study found that high levels of perceived control were associated with "high levels of job satisfaction, commitment, involvement, performance, and motivation and low levels of physical symptoms, emotional distress, role stress, absenteeism, intent to turnover, and turnover."[27] Since the pastor in my new situation expected that I knew what to do, I viewed my responsibilities as within my control and could decide how and what to prioritize in order to make progress in meeting my responsibilities.

"To do" lists, intertwined with meetings and the unexpected, can seem a mile long at first with every item appearing urgent. There are several strategies that help, providing space for the pastoral minister to maintain a sense of Christ-like service and to grow spiritually and emotionally.

1. **Set up a balanced and consistent routine.** Before I could prioritize my daily work, I needed to get everything down in one place where I could "see the big picture." This meant writing down deadlines, meeting times and locations, key contacts/resources, and needed information to develop a work schedule. Deciding on priorities became far simpler. It is like planning a road trip without a map: you eventually get where you plan to go but likely will spend more physical and mental energy and resources on unintended detours. In addition to mapping out the lay of the land, keeping a task list with essential information helps organize thoughts, evaluate options, and identify potential challenges.

2. **Establish effective time management practices.** Intentional use of available time helps prevent constant overload, chasing deadlines, and losing zest for what one is doing. My own disciplined use of time allows me to prioritize what to do and what is not possible given time constraints. I have choices! This is true for those with a different sense of time that emerges from their cultural heritage and background. The essence of time management is setting clear priorities *in light of important values* and then making choices and adjustments to meeting those priorities. The reward comes from feeling one can complete work in a timely fashion, stay engaged during important meetings, and open up space to be creative.

3. **Stay organized.** By prioritizing work that needs to get done, a person can identify those "quick hit" things that take only a bit of time, such as a phone call or reviewing a meeting agenda. This then allows a person to focus on time-sensitive items, items that necessitate more sustained involvement, or items requiring more relationship-building. Ultimately in my current position, I have twenty-four hours per week to dedicate to my ministry. Without an organized approach, I set myself up to be overwhelmed and not steward the allocated hours of my position. Moreover, lack of organization throws any hope for work-life balance to the winds. Having a clear picture of what needs to be done helps a person generate strategies to empower collaborative opportunities with parishioners or staff colleagues as well as discuss with the pastor or supervisor one's responsibilities and what may need to be adjusted in regard to expectations.

4. **Cultivate a sense of autonomy.** One of the biggest predictors of workplace satisfaction is the amount of autonomy that people have in their jobs.[28] Autonomy, simply put, is being in control of our experiences and actions because of options and choices. Higher levels of autonomy tend to result in an increase in independent thinking, job satisfaction, and better productivity. When people feel like their ideas and contributions matter, they are willing to contribute more regularly and with more effort. Micromanagement makes people feel unimportant and does not build trust. Rather, it creates insecurities. Certainly, the culture of an organization will play a significant role in whether the exercise of autonomy is valued. So too will one's sense of locus of control. "Cultivating autonomy" is significant because it means considering what one needs to do to address the issues in the organization that impede autonomy or to gain a more active internal sense of control.[29]

My new ministry setting, used as a reference point for this reflection, enabled me to make many of the decisions related to my responsibilities. I also experienced openness among co-workers where our work overlapped. The degree of actual autonomy might vary over time, but I perceived that I had choices, that my prior experience mattered, and I could control what I made of my situation. Beliefs about what controls our actions influence our behaviors and attitudes. This underlies self-efficacy or self-confidence—a conviction in our ability or chances of successfully accomplishing a task with a favorable outcome.[30] As Gandhi stated, "Your beliefs become your thoughts. Your thoughts become your words. Your words become your actions. Your actions become your habits. Your habits become your values. Your values become your destiny."[31] Bandura would add, "People with high assurance in their capabilities approach difficult tasks as challenges to be mastered rather than as threats to be avoided."[32]

While striving to grow and develop in providing the pastoral leadership needed in any ministerial setting, we return again and again to the source of our motivation. Work done in the course of ministry deepens a sense of personal accomplishment as we put our God-given talents and abilities to use. When our work helps others, it becomes a way to serve them. When we use our talents and abilities to help our organizations act to be healthier places to love, we serve the mission. What we do comes from God, so what we do might be a blessing to us and to others.

When that happens, we hopefully experience joy and contentment. As we are reminded in Philippians 4:13, "I have the strength for everything through him who empowers me." In ministry our senses of locus of control and self-efficacy, while important for our success and satisfaction, are not self-centered. They are powerful dispositions that enable us to accomplish with our ministry colleagues a great mission.

REWARD: RECOGNIZING THE DIGNITY OF WHAT WE DO

Kyle Lechtenberg

What happens when the systems in which we work seem indifferent to what we do and need to accomplish? Kyle Lechtenberg shared his own experience of this in his narrative. His essay is helpful by elaborating what real reward means in the context of ministerial practice and its significance in creating a healthy workplace.

Reward in the ministerial workplace is evident primarily by its intangible characteristics—the affirmations or support that help lay ecclesial ministers know they are doing a good job, are valued members of a team, and are making a positive contribution to the organization. Whatever the ministry setting, they are all founded after the command and model of Jesus. Intangible rewards can be expressed by the organization through things like continuing education, conference attendance, celebrations after major events, private and public recognition of the individual's contribution to the life of the organization.

Reward can also come at times when the minister needs growth or improvement, or when conflict arises. How does the leader dignify the minister by addressing concerns with performance? What is the plan to approach and resolve conflict, whether it is between peers or people at different levels of responsibility? How does parish ministry nourish or enliven faith in God, faith of the minister himself or herself rippling outward from that person's ministry? How does it reflect and develop his or her unique baptismal gifts? Authentically expressed rewards need to be thoroughly interwoven in ministry as part of how the organization—

parish or other ministry setting—contributes to the health and vitality of both the individual minister and the organization itself.

I now understand the primary reward I seek is a place to flourish with my own God-given gifts and that raises up everyone's area of ministry. Standing in the midst of the worshiping people of God is where I belong, leading and assisting those who lead our Church's liturgical prayer. The tradition and teaching of the Church, the holy Scriptures, and the Spirit moving in my heart and soul affirm this as well as the supportive networks of friends, family, and other Christians who care when I am weighed down by fear, doubt, and isolation.

The AMC Series *Mad Men* is set in 1960s New York City and explores the rise of today's advertising culture and its effects on people, relationships, and the competition for new consumers. The following is a heated exchange between Don Draper, head of the department, and Peggy Olson, a young up-and-coming creative mind. Peggy is looking for recognition for her hard work and creativity on a project. Don had earned a Clio Award for excellence in television advertising. The scene plays out like this:

DON: There are no credits on commercials.

PEGGY: But you got the Clio!

DON: It's your job! I give you money, you give me ideas.

PEGGY: And you never say thank you.

DON: That's what the money is for! You're young. You will get your recognition. And honestly, it is absolutely ridiculous to be two years into your career and counting your ideas. Everything to you is an opportunity. And you should be thanking me every morning when you wake up, along with Jesus, for giving you another day!

Peggy begins to cry.

DON: Oh, come on.

Peggy turns to walk out of Don's office.[33]

Employee expectations of reward have come a long way since the 1960s. In a 2008 article in the *Journal for Business Ethics*, the authors present research on the effects of organizational spirituality with rewards on worker satisfaction. The authors learned that, when an organization operates out of a sense of spirituality (practicing values such as connectedness, meaning, purpose, altruism, virtue, nurturance, and hope), worker satisfaction with intrinsic and extrinsic rewards (promotions, recognition, a sense of achievement) was higher. To today's Don Drapers, in whatever field of employment, it does matter that you say "Thank you" because your workers want more than just the money.[34]

My experience and theological studies help me to see that my unique set of skills, knowledge, and passions for the liturgy combined with a desire to lead people in prayer and release their talents for worship landed me squarely in the worshipping Body of Christ. I find joy in opening the gifts of a choir, which, in turn, opens the voice of a singing assembly. I have been effective in this role in several communities, and I now understand it as a calling or vocation, something *Co-workers in the Vineyard of the Lord* acknowledges: "These lay ecclesial ministers often express a sense of being called. This sense motivates what they are doing, guiding and shaping a major life choice and commitment to Church ministry."[35]

Perhaps the closest equivalent to "that's what the money's for!" in the ministerial setting is, "You'll get your reward in heaven!" Sometimes this is used as a joke among ministry people, ordained and lay ecclesial. Sometimes, it is used to justify long hours, little recognition, unachievable workloads, or denying needed resources. If we would instead look to the idea of our Christian life as a foretaste of the feast to come, we don't need to rely solely on a reward given after death! We can expect to experience that today, in our worship of God and in the way we relate with one another that is rooted in our baptism and in the communion of the trinitarian life of God.

As a lay ecclesial minister, who has worked for eighteen years in full-time ministry while acquiring a graduate theological degree, the primary reward I seek is to know that my place around the table of the Eucharist and in the parish office are really one and the same. Participating in the Eucharist is our "right and duty" by reason of our baptism.[36] Flowing from that is the reality that God has called me into the light and life of Jesus Christ and his Church in a way that is completely unique, varied, and validated by the community. I seek the reward of working with clergy and lay ecclesial ministers who understand each other's unique stations in life. A celibate pastor, supported materially and intangibly by the parish and diocese, has very different needs than

Creating a New Story

a lay ecclesial minister seeking to make a living and life while, in many cases, supporting a family and growing a marriage.

Let us reorient our conversation about "who can do what" in ministerial settings and point more overtly toward Christ, the head of the Church. When ministry is done in relation to the Eucharist, our attention can be redirected to focus more clearly on the One who calls everyone to share in some way in his mission to bring salvation and eternal life to the entire world.

A common theme in this exploration of reward in the ministerial setting is dignity. Some of my past experiences have resulted in the silencing or quieting of my dignity as a worker. Another strain on individual dignity is having rewards withheld or given under false pretenses. The Church quenches the Spirit when lay ecclesial ministers are feared, silenced, controlled, shamed, or undervalued by clergy or laypersons in positions of authority. In contrast, the Church ignites the Spirit when these ministers are supported, uplifted, valued with material and intangible rewards of compensation, reasonable working hours, appropriate esteem, and kindness, and seen as true co-workers, not just with the ordained, but like them, with Christ. In each of my ministerial settings, even the ones with painful difficulties, I found ways to thrive. I have experienced the Spirit and my spirit to be unbounded and free when I pursue creative musical outlets, follow my attraction to interfaith and ecumenical prayer, lead a parish through a church dedication, or help a parish to liturgically say farewell to a much-loved pastor at his retirement.

At first, I was surprised when much of the conversation and resources around the project for this book centered on burnout. I heard myself murmuring, "I'm not burned out; I'm just having some troubles connecting with people. I'm not burned out; I just need to get more organized and focused. I'm not burned out; I just have a lot of personal difficulties and stresses right now." Burnout isn't exclusively a dramatic implosion or explosion that results in leaving or being asked to leave a job, ministerial or otherwise. Christiana Maslach and Michael Leiter's book *Banishing Burnout* explores the reality of burnout for those in "helping" professions in many facets. According to Maslach and Leiter, burnout is lost energy, lost enthusiasm, and lost confidence.[37] Across my career in ministry, the way intangible rewards such as recognition, continuing education, and flexibility in hours were withheld or given to me or colleagues wore on me. In some cases, I was the "winner" who got plenty of extras while another staff member did not. In others, I was the one on the outside of the favored group.

Banishing Burnout has a helpful way of framing the issue: there are steps we can take to improve our relationship with our ministry. When our awareness is clouded or darkened by any degree of burnout, it can be difficult to understand that there are things we can do as individual ministers. This is surely the case when we look at something like reward.

Employers within and outside ministry settings are recognizing that a more holistic reward structure cultivates and sustains employees who are happier, healthier, and more willing to extend themselves for the benefit of the organization. Nonmonetary (beyond the paycheck) compensation takes a variety of forms: flexible work hours/options to work from home; generous and flexible paid time off; paid parental leave; compensation packages that provide for medical coverage and retirement contributions; fitness challenges/gym memberships; team social events; floating holiday(s) such as one's birthday; continuing education budget; conference attendance or skill building; staff retreat or recreation days; public or private recognition of family supports necessary for successful ministry (e.g., spouse takes on childcare on Church holidays or at parish events); and building a culture that people want to be a part of by respecting each individual and their ministry's area of unique needs, style, and contribution.

Every organization will likely not do every one of these items, and they may change through the years as employee needs change and grow. If a religious organization is relying on the idea that Church work is reward enough, and the paycheck they give them is already beyond what they deserve (since lay ministry could easily be done by energized volunteers), culture and morale suffer, and ministry employees lose interest in supporting the organization. If, on the other hand, genuine efforts are made to recognize that ministers desire and need more than a paycheck, then culture and morale can thrive. Rewarding minister employees beyond the paycheck for their contribution and sacrifices, through means mentioned above and other creative approaches, can engender a loyalty and commitment to the mission of the organization that will outweigh the costs of developing and providing these rewards.

Creating a New Story

WORKLOAD: THE CHALLENGE OF BALANCE
Yaret Macedo

> Yaret Macedo's narrative might leave readers breathless in terms of the scale of activity she encountered in her workplace. But we all know what happens as ministerial programs and responsibilities seem to constantly expand. There is more to do with less time, personnel, and resources. In this essay, the author provides a framework for considering balance in the workplace that represents more than a wish but flows from how we understand mission and ministry.

Hispanic people make up one of the largest ethnic groups in the United States. According to Hosffman Ospino, "Twenty-five percent of all Catholic parishes intentionally serve Hispanics."[38] This translates into significantly increased efforts to address the needs that Hispanic communities present. There are sixty-two parishes in the Diocese of Orange, and many offer at least one Mass in Spanish. My parish (Immaculate Heart of Mary) has one of the highest Hispanic concentrations in the Diocese of Orange with about seven thousand registered households that total twenty-five thousand individuals. The pastoral needs in such a large parish include fostering a Catholic identity, attending to people's spiritual, sacramental, and social needs, and above all, working with limited resources.[39] With the large influx of immigrant families, the community walks with them in their daily struggles—immigration issues, low incomes, housing issues, medical and educational needs. The complexity of my workload and those of other pastoral leaders increases as we serve a community that is a spiritual home for two distinct ethnic cultures: 90 percent are Hispanic, and 10 percent are Vietnamese.

Right before the 2020 pandemic, our church building was filled to capacity at each weekend Mass. The church was open seven days a week from 9:00 a.m. to 9:00 p.m. with two daily Masses, weekly evening adoration, two days of reconciliation, and three to five different group gatherings per night. In addition, other sacraments and liturgies were celebrated as needed—baptisms, funerals, *quinceañeras*, individual and group weddings, anniversaries, and cultural group Masses honoring a saint from a specific region of Mexico or other Latin-American country.

During the pandemic, our church closed its doors, ministers went home, and most of our employees left on furlough. Just the pastor, two parochial vicars, and I held things together. Working from home on a reduced salary and on call, I needed to respond to every emergency, voicemail, and email from parishioners as well as manage the calendar. I am confronted with the turmoil of events, emotions, and uncertainty over what the new reality of pastoral work will be like in the future.

Workload is not only defined by tasks I do daily. It is marshalling financial resources and tending to the emotional work of accompanying a multicultural community and intercultural encounters. Bret Hoover, in *The Shared Parish*, writes, "Contact across cultures disturbs the psychological equilibrium of persons involved. Intercultural encounter creates both uncertainty and anxiety."[40] In addition, accompanying this parish community involves emotional situations, personal confrontations, one-on-one conversations, and conflict resolutions. The workload in ministry that comes from being attentive to the people's needs is part of embracing the cross of Jesus for his people. However, some balanced and realistic perspectives are necessary to maintain healthier ministers.

The 2010 study "Average Household Weekly Offertory by Parish Ethnic Composition" indicates that the average weekly family offering in all parishes was $9.43. In a parish with more than 50 percent Hispanic members, the weekly offertory is $5.59.[41] Parish financial and physical resources are limited so groups often subsidize most of their own expenses through fundraising. Like St. Paul, who avoided imposing himself on the communities, our pastoral leaders do not wish to be a burden on fledgling Christian communities nor impose themselves on the communities. Indeed, Paul reminds the Christian community at Thessalonica that "nor did we eat food received free from anyone. On the contrary, in toil and drudgery, night and day we worked, so as not to burden any of you" (2 Thess 3:8). Keeping our staff small and expenses down are necessities as we meet our daily financial needs. Yet we face the challenge of gauging which services should be provided and at what expense while balancing our income. Idleness is not our way of life!

According to Christina Maslach in the *Burnout Toolkit for Human Services Individual Report*, "Workload is the amount of work to be done in a given time. A manageable workload provides the opportunity to do what you enjoy, to pursue career objectives, and to develop professionally. A crisis in workload is not just stretching to meet a new challenge but going beyond human limits. For example, a person does not have time to do the work that must be done."[42] In many instances, due to the demand for services, time, and resources, clergy, lay staff, and group leaders often find themselves stretched thin as they try to accomplish their tasks.

Three key elements influence the workload culture of a local parish: (1) the commitment of staff ministers rooted in their baptismal call, (2) the importance of fostering a healthy spiritual life to create effective staff ministers, and (3) the need for an ecclesiology of communion between clergy and lay ministers.

Baptismal Call

According to *Co-workers in the Vineyard of the Lord*, "All of the baptized are called to work toward the transformation of the world." This transformation happens through a diversity of ministries, each essential to respond to the pastoral needs of the people. These ministries are composed of baptized ministers who are disciples of Jesus Christ and flow from the Spirit of God who transforms individual gifts and talents for service to the Gospel. Ministers, therefore, serve with a clear purpose because a "ministry is both a religious and a moral enterprise."[43] Following St. Paul's affirmation in 1 Corinthians 12:4–7, the Holy Spirit gives gifts and charisms to every baptized person. However, these charisms are not for their own benefit. It is everyone's responsibility to put the gifts that were given to work in their specific ministry for the common good of the Church.

My experience as a disciple over the last twenty years prepared me for my current position and confirms my vocational calling, rooted in baptism, to be a lay ecclesial minister in the name of the Church. My vision of ministry is a community of giftedness inspired by the Holy Spirit. My involvement began with a charismatic renewal (*Renovación Carismática*) prayer group at my childhood parish. There I received the gift of accompaniment at the age of thirteen. It was the first time I felt loved and accepted by God and by a group of people who accepted me with little knowledge of who I was. This call to ministry began a new way of life, a deepening in a spirituality of stewardship where I understood that it was a responsibility to use my gifts and talents in service to my community.

Over the years, I have served in different capacities, first as a volunteer and later as a paid lay minister. In my charismatic prayer group,

I served in different ministries and received new opportunities to use my evolving leadership skills, including how to delegate tasks to others. Throughout these years of service, I have understood that the "moral responsibilities of being a pastoral minister arise ultimately from the call of God to love in ways that reflect what being a disciple of Jesus demands of us in the practice of ministry."[44] My eyes and heart are big when it comes to seeing the needs of the community. My background provided the necessary knowledge I would need as director and my familiarity with the parish equipped me with an insider's awareness of its needs and challenges. My preparation was invaluable, but I had not calculated the cost to my spiritual life. There was a point where I got lost trying to balance my ministerial life. I would often feel very discombobulated with little space for prayer.

Healthy Spiritual Life

A new hire is expected to have ministry experience and be knowledgeable in their respective work areas to better serve this community. My ultimate goal for these committed and enthusiastic newly hired individuals is that they give their best to every parishioner. I have come to learn that in this fast-paced, face-to-face work environment, parish staff are confronted with daily situations that can bring them to the edge of burnout. It is not because they do not love their ministry and the people they accompany, but because there is no breathing space. According to Christina Maslach, "Burnout is a syndrome of emotional exhaustion (lost energy), depersonalization (lost enthusiasm), and reduced personal accomplishment (lost confidence) that can occur among individuals who do 'people-work' of some kind."[45] These past four years working at my parish have been filled with deadlines to accomplish the goals I saw necessary to strengthen parish vibrancy. We were it—a pastor, two parochial vicars, three part-time deacons, and four full-time lay ecclesial ministers. With limited financial resources, we felt blessed with the part-time support staff we had.

I was busy with so many things! Work, however, was never a problem for me. I grew up in a family in which working to survive was normal. My mother, a single parent raising three children, always had her nose to the grindstone. I developed a habit of having more deadlines than lifelines. I needed freedom from the tyranny of the urgent. Ministers reach the burnout point due to overwork. This hinders their personal wholeness because excessive work robs the leisure needed for balanced living.[46] In addition, if ministers have not resolved their personal and human development issues, they can easily experience some of the ministerial dysfunctions identified by Thomas W. Frazier, such as lack of balance, fulfillment of unmet needs, underdeveloped ministerial identity, external locus of control, and perpetuation of dysfunction.[47] According to Frazier, the interaction of personal dysfunction with dysfunctional aspects of ministerial work affects the wellness and effectiveness of the minister.[48] These dysfunctional aspects of ministry hinder the growth of a healthy spiritual life because of the complexity of ministry.

One of the most common aspects of dysfunction in ministry is the lack of balance in the personal and work lives of minsters because of the "inflated sense of mission without a realistic assessment of the limitations."[49] In *Flourishing in Ministry: How to Cultivate Clergy Wellbeing*, Matt Bloom describes the burden of ministry as high-stakes work; it is complex, continuous, and diverse, punctuated by unexpected events. There is little structure or guidance for prioritizing ministry work, a reliance on more digital and less in-person communication, and rapid external change.[50] Overlooking chronic fatigue, ministers just press on and come to a point where they lose a sense of themselves by not attending to their eating habits, exercise, hobbies, or relationships with God and others. They tend to end each workday exhausted.

Ministers often focus more on quantity than quality. We get trapped in the numbers game in which the number of people at any given event seems more important than how lives are transformed and turned toward Christ. Jesus paid attention to people. For example, in his encounter with the woman at the well, his compassion and empathy made it possible for the woman to feel welcomed, appreciated, and loved.

One way of fostering a healthy spiritual life among ministers is by helping them find balance. Individual balance is important and can be cultivated by noticing these areas: stimulation and quiet, reflection and action; work and leisure; self-care and care of others, self-improvement and patience, future aspirations and present positive realities, involvement and detachment.[51] In short, it is important to foster a healthy spiritual life by imitating Jesus's life where he was able to find a "rhythm of holiness that included time for ministry, for withdrawal, and for relaxing in the congenial company of friends" in order to create effective ministers to work for the Church.[52]

Communion Ecclesiology

When ministers respond to their call through their "diverse ministries and charisms," they are carrying out the mission of the Church in an ecclesiology of communion.[53] Communion ecclesiology responds to the "actual reality of the ministries" through the sacramental and pastoral life of the Church because it gives the opportunity to the people of God to serve in a specific ministry where they are called and recognized.[54] For instance, clergy and lay ministers are called to carry out the mission of the Church as servant leaders. According to Richard R. Osmer, "Servant leadership is leadership that influences the congregation to change in a way that more fully embodies the servanthood of Christ."[55] Osmer describes three forms of servant leadership: task competence, transactional leadership, and transforming leadership.[56] In *task competence*, the most important thing is that leaders imitate Jesus's humbleness, realizing that they cannot do everything by themselves and that they depend on others to carry out the mission. In *transactional leadership*, leaders create a place where the needs of people are met in return for their support and participation in accomplishing the mission—a form of holding people accountable for the ministry in which they serve.[57] Finally, *transforming leadership* is a process of deep change that imitates Christ's suffering in the sense that in order to become good leaders, they must go through the hardships of leading. This means that transforming leaders must take risks, empower others, and not get attached to their ministries as this would prevent them from being objective in their decision-making.

There have been instances where staff or volunteer ministers, including clergy, have overstepped each other's roles or ministries which caused damage to the working relationships. When relationships are damaged, the entire work dynamic falls through the cracks because no one takes responsibility for their own actions. We begin to have negative views of people, wanting to do everything by ourselves and not willing to be of service to others. I am convinced that if we truly understand and implement collaboration and servant leadership qualities, our work environment and ministries can be strengthened. At the same time, this model of collaboration and leadership can help nurture our diverse gifts and give time and space to a shared ministry where everyone can fulfill their responsibilities without experiencing burnout.

To foster effective ministers, parishes and diocesan offices need to collaborate in giving a place to an "ordered, relational, ministerial community"[58] between clergy and lay ministers. Then service, relationship, and accountability from the ministers will be created because, according to Edward P. Hahnenberg, "ministry is a relational reality."[59] Furthermore, clergy and lay ministries would gain more if they collaborate, forming genuine partnerships and fostering relationships of trust and productive working relationships at the parish level.[60] The parish, as a whole, would benefit because it would not only improve the parish's response to the pastoral needs, but it could become a vibrant parish.[61] Vibrancy comes when leadership imitates Jesus as a servant leader and serves a communion of ministries that welcomes everyone to experience the richness of being a part of the Church.

FAIRNESS: PRACTICING JUSTICE, SHOWING CARE

Timothy Johnston

With clarity and transparency, Timothy Johnston tells us in his narrative his own struggles when confronted with the effects of a lack of fairness. The feelings that emerge when one is treated unfairly are often disorienting and discouraging. In his essay, Timothy steps back from the immediacy of his story to take a broader look at the issue of fairness and what it requires from organizations and individuals in those organizations.

How many times have you heard someone say, "That's not fair"? Parents and teachers hear it more often than they can count. Organizations experience the same sentiment in their employees. A review of the literature often defines *fairness* as an equitable exchange, that is, what we get for what we give. However, experience tells us that fairness is more than just equal treatment; fairness also encompasses how we are treated as compared to others. *Fairness* is the "impartial and just treatment or behavior without favoritism or discrimination."[62] Fairness is more than practicing justice; it is also about care.

Where does the responsibility for fairness in an organization rest? Is it with the supervisor? Is it with the employee? Bruce Weinstein in *The Good Ones: Ten Crucial Qualities of High-Character Employees*, writes, "Fairness has three major applications at work: allocating scarce resources appropriately…disciplining people the right way; and turning unjust situations into just ones."[63] Fairness is not appraised based on the scales of justice alone. Transformational leadership has proven more effective than transactional leadership when it comes to winning commitment and earning the trust of followers. Transactional leadership focuses on issues of exchange—this for that. Within transformational leadership, there is an element called "consideration." Followers perceive that the leader truly cares about them, and, more generally, demonstrates this in policy and behavior.

"The tipping point for burnout is fairness," writes William P. Macaux in *Engagement, Fairness and Care*.[64] Of the six risk factors, the one that has proven most predictive of burnout or engagement, is fairness. In a longitudinal study, those who reported incongruity in the area of fairness moved from an unstable status to one of burnout. Just as important, those who experienced their workplace and their supervisor as fair moved toward engagement.

Fair processes or *fair outcomes* are benchmarks by which the concept of fairness is measured. For example, at a newly clustered Catholic community, there is going to be a staff reorganization. The lay ecclesial ministers assess the *fairness of this process* with these questions:

1. Will diocesan and parish leaders invite us to participate in the decision-making process?

2. Will our expertise and experience be given serious consideration in the pastoral planning?

3. By what method will decisions be made and evaluated?

4. Will this process remain consistent throughout the reorganization?

5. Is the decision-making process transparent?

6. Are the personal biases of the decision-maker acknowledged and minimized?

7. Do the decision makers explain why a decision is made?

8. Do they treat the pastoral leaders respectfully, actively listening to their concerns and empathizing with their points of view?

Creating a New Story

9. Is ample advance notice given if and when a position is eliminated or redefined?

Outcome fairness is different. For example, a lay ecclesial minister applies for a new open position in the area Catholic community. He does not get the position; however, he believes the chosen candidate was qualified, and his supervisor had a candid discussion with him about how he can be better prepared for the next opportunity. Because he felt seen and acknowledged, he will be a lot more productive and engaged than if he believes the person who got the job was the boss's favorite or if he received no guidance on how to move forward.

But what about me? As a young boy, I saw the world in black and white terms. I required that rules be applied equally to classmates, siblings, and even the wider world. Eventually, my colleagues would face the same expectations. When rules aren't followed, parameters are breached, and shared policies aren't obeyed or enforced, I tend to become discontent and irritable to the point that I find myself acting mean-spirited and deceptively righteous. I'd think to myself, "Of course, I am honorable. I follow the rules and work harder, longer, and produce more results." Upon much reflection, it became clear that much of this angst was rooted in my need for approval and acceptance.

Through reflection, I learned, and could admit, that I was in an unhealthy pattern and, consequently, this unhealthy and damaging pattern led to unhappiness and irritability. I had to recognize where my sense of fairness stemmed from and why it was like a burning fire within me. I needed to learn why it becomes easy for me to develop a poor opinion of these "rebel" co-workers. When I was upset about how unfairly the rules were applied or resources were distributed, it was easy for me to paint the picture that they could do nothing right; I actively worked at disliking them.[65] Reflecting on my narrative for this book has revealed that my definition and practice of fairness has not evolved much as my ministry developed, but how I respond and engage has changed.

In my first years in ministry, justice or fairness consumed a lot of my energy, even with what some would call trivial matters. For example, if Ava got X number of vacation days, I too felt I should be granted X number of vacation days, no matter the discrepancy in seniority. It was only fair. If George was able to come in late every morning without repercussions, then why wasn't I rewarded for always being prompt? Could I too come in late and not be reprimanded? It was only fair. I'd ask, "Why is my office budget significantly less than office X?" It was only fair if each office had the same budget to do the necessary work. My sense of fairness, at the time, led me to believe that the rules should be applied equally to everyone because we all had the same employee handbook and the same responsibilities (even if in different specialties) with the goal of serving God's people.

As I've wrestled with fairness in my ministry, three Scripture passages have accompanied me and provided insight to my circumstances. First, is the story of the prodigal son (Luke 15:1–3, 11–32). In this familiar story, while I appreciate its forgiveness motif, I am caught up with the story of the older brother who stayed and worked hard. When I've sat with this story, I find myself in conversation with him and empathizing with his anger (v. 28). Didn't he deserve a celebration for not squandering his inheritance and staying to support the work of his father? Why is the younger brother rewarded for his spendthrift behavior? This part of the Gospel always grabbed my attention, even as a young child. Like the older brother who witnessed his father's magnanimous gesture toward the reckless brother, my narrative recounts how I perceived the act of distributing the profits from an event among various offices as unjust and imprudent. To me, it seemed like a reward for the others who didn't assist with the event. In my own theological reflection, as I've continued to dialogue with the older brother in the parable, he shared with me that it took a long time for him to understand the generosity of his father; the father wasn't rewarding his prodigal son, but out of love welcoming him back into the fold and celebrating the lessons learned.

Second is the story of the workers in the vineyard (Matt 20:1–6). Barbara Reid says, "In the story the first hired are paid last because the point of the story depends on their seeing what the last hired received.... Does not justice demand that those who worked more earn more?"[66] Reid's question is my question; along with the first hired, I grumble at what seems unjust. In my narrative, I see myself and the team as the first hired, and my colleague who complained as the last to be hired. Of course, I grumbled at the thought he would receive remuneration for work to which he didn't contribute. All these years later, it is a bit easier to step back and reassess the situation.

Prayer with this passage has helped me broaden my horizon and, if you will, see between the lines. What I was blind to in those early years of ministry was the fact that the management team did have the well-being of the whole organization at heart, even if it was not clearly communicated. They truly felt that the distribution of the funds would benefit more people in the end and, therefore, benefit the whole Church. Reid puts this into perspective:

> In God's realm, justice means that all are fed as a sign of God's equal and inclusive love; it does not mean getting what we deserve, either in terms of retribution for wrongdoing or recompense for good deeds…[by focusing] on their perceived loss…[the grumblers] miss the limitless goodness and generosity of the landowner.[67]

Exactly! Like the grumblers, I focused on my loss and was blind to the fact that the abundant gift we received could be shared with my colleagues for the good of the whole.

The third Scripture passage is Proverbs 29:11. According to Katherine M. Hayes, this passage provides sayings on the impact of the just (wise) and the wicked (foolish) on society.[68] This wisdom can also be applied to the ministerial workplace. Praying with the phrase "A fool gives full vent to anger" (NRSV) has given me a new perspective on how I respond when I experience unfairness. I learned that my venting lacks productivity; it riles others instead of being constructive and working toward conflict resolution. The proverb teaches that the wise hold back. This is not a silent passivity; it allows for prudent assessment that leads to informed resolutions and processes.

Another wisdom source is *The Rule of St. Benedict*. In the Prologue, Benedict introduces the concept of *aequitas*, in other words, doing "what is proper, giving each one what he is entitled to or needs, not simply a rigid application of the law to individuals, but consideration of the personal situation."[69] In this, we see Benedict's recognition of the importance of the common dignity of each community member as well as his individuality and uniqueness. The *Rule* understands that a healthy community values genuine respect for each person who comprises it.

In chapter 2 of his *Rule*, Benedict describes the qualities of the abbot. From this, we learn that a leader, who follows the *Rule*, is one who has real authority, but is also just and reasonable and settles "everything with foresight and fairness" (RB 3.6, emphasis added). Benedict notes that the abbot was to respect the diversity of individuals within the community: accommodating and adapting "himself to each one's character and intelligence [so] that he will not only keep…[those already] entrusted to his care from dwindling but will rejoice in the increase" in new members (*RB* 2.32).[70] Benedict's instruction respects the needs of each person and requires discernment by the abbot regarding a person or a situation. The monastic superior must lead and guide with discretion; this value holds true today for anyone in Church ministry.

The wisdom we find in the *Rule of St. Benedict* is one of dialogue and discernment. For example, when the superior makes a decision with which the monk struggles, the monk has two opportunities to discuss it further with the abbot. Only then, when the abbot has made his final decision, would the monk obey and follow through, "trusting in God's help" (*RB* 68:4–5). There is implicit here a "strong sense of contextuality."[71] What is a good decision in one context may not be in another. Benedict recognized that change was a part of life. The quality of spiritual discernment was (and is) essential to recognize when one should have priority over another. To preserve community harmony within this process, Benedict also says to reach out, not only to the whole community, but also to its younger members since their views can be invaluable (*RB* 3:1–3). Here, the *Rule*'s spirit of moderation is evident; it is constantly to be applied "according to the dictates of equity" (*RB* Prol. 47).

In conclusion, Jill Schiefelbein provides important advice:

> As humans, we want to be treated equitably. We want to know that we're valued, that our work matters, and that we are compensated fairly for our efforts. The concept of equity involves looking at a situation and identifying the variables—the people involved, the resources at play and the situational factors—and then asking yourself these questions:
>
> 1. Are we giving each person the necessary resources?
> 2. Are we giving each person a proportional amount of attention?
> 3. Are we showing appreciation in a balanced way?
> 4. Are we giving each person an equal opportunity to succeed?[72]

Schiefelbein concisely articulates many of the same principles found in the *Rule of St. Benedict* and the real experiences we all desire in our ministerial setting. In seeking fairness, we seek respect, to be heard, to be seen, and to be valued. What Scripture and the *Rule* help us see is that fairness implies a deep reverence for the person, authentic discernment and dialogue, and a culture of trust.

FINANCIAL WELL-BEING: THE COSTS OF VOCATIONAL CALL

Jim Wahl

In his compelling narrative, Jim Wahl situated financial well-being for a lay ecclesial minister squarely in the center of a personal family crisis. In his essay, Jim makes clear that his situation simply dramatizes a reality that has far wider implications for the economic well-being of those serving the Church that go to the very root of the Church's own profound commitment to justice. Jim acknowledges the financial well-being of a lay ecclesial minister is dependent on Sunday offertory collections that are diminishing. At the same time, he does not find that fact sufficient to warrant abandoning the clear principles of justice as they apply to the needs of the Church's lay ecclesial ministers.

In 2013, Pope Francis exhorted in *Evangelii Gaudium* that people today "thirst for authenticity."[73] He then named what will not satisfy this thirst: an economy of exclusion, the new idolatry of money, a financial system that rules rather than serves, and an inequality that spawns violence.[74] Revisiting the events of three years ago in the opening narrative has allowed me to begin asking questions of myself. Why were my feelings so visceral? Why, when so much of the community was rallying around my family in our urgent needs, would the response of one individual bring such anxiety and feelings of betrayal? Why could I not simply steer conversations back to the overall budget question and alleviate the pastor's concern? In essence, I am thirsting for authenticity.

Reflecting on these questions has brought clarity about the covenant relationship between the Church as employer and the minister as employee. This covenant is not clearly indicated in the job description for my position nor was it explicitly stated when I interviewed. Covenant language has not been spoken in the few times I've been formally evaluated nor is it used when I've received changes to salary or other human resource benefits. And yet it has been at the foundation of my response to God's call to serve the Church. Covenant undergirds the entirety of my investment of time and talent in my ministry, calling me to continue to explore the skills and education I need to competently serve the people of God. I believe the implicit, unwritten covenant drove the community to respond financially and emotionally to my family's needs on multiple occasions. As expressed in the U.S. bishops' 1992 pastoral letter *Stewardship: A Disciple's Response*, in a eucharistic community, all the faithful "reaffirm their participation in the New Covenant; they give thanks to God for blessings received; and they strengthen their bonds of commitment to one another as members of the covenant community Jesus forms." I experienced the pastor's disconnection to my emotional and financial needs as a betrayal of this covenant.

Unfortunately, as a lay ecclesial minister, I have heard and witnessed many such betrayals: thoughtless or reactive terminations, failure to address inequities in salary, an indifference to the need for sustainable retirement and health benefits, and a lack of follow through on educational benefits or reimbursement, to name a few. While as a Church we are not necessarily comparable to other institutions and face many growing financial challenges, we must ensure that all ministers, ordained and lay alike, are treated with justice and fairness. Movement toward a relationship of covenant between the Church and its lay ecclesial ministers will require a reflection on many of our current human resource practices in light of national practices, the needs of lay ministers, and the prophetic call of our tradition itself.

I began working in the Church during college, nearly thirty years ago. I recall, at that time, conversations about my employment with other Church professionals and ministers, the term *contract* was often used. However, this confused me. I have never had a contract working for the Church. I was well aware of "at-will" employment as I also worked in the banking industry early in my career and used that term in all formal human resource processes. What I soon recognized was that, at some point, many parishes and dioceses had moved away from the idea of contract with its lay ecclesial ministers and adopted the standard practice of the business world: at-will employment.

The use of at-will employment has become normative for many dioceses and nearly all parish employees. A 2015 report by the Center for Applied Research in the Apostolate at Georgetown University (CARA) indicated that only 17 percent of U.S. dioceses reported that most of the lay ecclesial ministers in their employ had contracts.[75] Sadly, the use of at-will employment is often recognized in the United States as simply the way of employment. What is not recognized is that this is not normative worldwide but is a product of late nineteenth-century capitalism.[76] Ironically, local churches have adopted the practices that Leo XIII was responding to when he wrote the encyclical *Rerum Novarum*: "And it is for this reason that wage-earners, since they mostly belong in the mass of the needy, should be specially cared for and protected by the government."[77] In fact, the U.S. bishops, in *Co-workers in the Vineyard of the Lord*, seemingly adopt the need for at-will employment to accommodate changes in parish leadership: "It may be desirable in some situations that the term of a lay ecclesial minister conclude, even if subject to renewal, when the pastor's term of office comes to an end."[78] This contradicts an earlier statement that lay ecclesial ministers will continue in such service over time.[79]

As a director of music in the Church for over twenty years, I have benefited from not only the work of pioneers in musical liturgy since the days of the Second Vatican Council, but also from a tradition of professional music ministry in the history of the Church. The same CARA report identified earlier lists the median income for directors of liturgy and music at $67,000 per year. However, when the role of liturgy is removed from the job position, the corresponding median pay is $52,000. A continuing reduction in median income is reflected in various job titles: catechetical ministry director $38,025, youth ministry director $34,940, RCIA director $33,600, youth minister $30,520.[80] To put these salaries in perspective, the 2020 federal poverty level for a family of four is $26,200. Twenty-seven percent of lay ecclesial ministers surveyed in 2012 reported ministry and income wages at or below the poverty level for a family of four in that year.[81] Clearly the standardization of salaries is necessary, particularly in elevating the role and remuneration for those involved in the formation of youth. The work of the Alliance for the Certification of Lay Ministers in setting standards of certification is instrumental in this effort but must be joined by a commitment from the U.S. Conference of Catholic Bishops to value the work of lay ecclesial ministries with a just salary.[82]

However, salary, even if adjusted for cost of living, is not the only metric to be considered when measuring financial well-being. Further studies should look at the availability of retirement plans, including the percentage employees contributing, the average percentage of annual income contributed, and the number of loans or early withdrawals against the plan. A national survey that evaluates employee perceptions in terms of pay, benefits, and security would be extremely helpful.[83] In addition, a crucial element in need of further research is healthcare expenses. These costs, an area of critical national concern, are particularly relevant to lay ecclesial ministers, particularly in light of the salary injustices identified above.

In his 1981 encyclical on human work, St. John Paul II expressed the urgency of adequate health care for workers and their families: besides wages, various social benefits intended to ensure the life and health of workers and their families play a part here. The expenses involved in healthcare, especially in the case of accidents at work, demand that medical assistance should be easily available for workers, and that as far as possible it should be cheap or even free of charge.[84] While the 2015 CARA report included a survey of health benefits, this was incomplete and urgently in need of further research. My own anecdotal experience is that coverage for dependents, including spouses, is woefully inadequate compared to other industries, and is often reflective of plans that are designed with the needs of priests, seminarians, and religious as primary concerns, obviously lessening the need for dependent coverage. Finally, long-term disability is a benefit that is not included in the 2015 CARA report, and more research is necessary to ensure that those who have responded to a vocation to serve the Church are not left without resources in case of a long-term illness.

As anyone who has worked in lay ecclesial ministry for several years learns, those who enter the vineyard of ecclesial ministry are graced with the desire to learn more about their ministry and their tradition. Graduate theological education or a diocesan certification process is necessary to gain the competencies for ministry in diocesan and parish ministry as outlined by the USCCB in *Co-Workers in the Vineyard of the Lord*. CARA reports that over one-third of lay ecclesial ministers surveyed have a master's degree or are in the process of obtaining the degree.[85] However, compared to other ecclesial leaders, namely, seminarian and deacon aspirants, there is a lack of equity in formation. Those on track for ordination are typically assured the privilege of having their diocese and parish support their education and formation. Most lay ecclesial ministers, on the other hand, often depend on partial scholarships for tuition and fund the remaining amount. Some fund the entire cost themselves. Incurring such education debt saddles the financial well-being of lay ecclesial ministers when they accept positions with salaries that are not comparable to their professional preparation. More research is needed on the ratio of educational debt to income for lay ecclesial ministers and how this relates to other vocations.

Finally, while my experience as a lay ecclesial minister provides a certain and needed lens to view financial well-being, it is imperative that we also look at the larger organizational structures that shape the financial conditions for parishes today. Undoubtedly, there has been a substantial shift in the parish workforce over the past fifty years. Where once parishes were staffed almost entirely by clergy and vowed religious, today they are staffed primarily by the laity, many with advanced degrees and the need for compensation in line with their professional status. This comes with a cost. The largest expense in parish budgets is salary and benefits, an average of 39 percent of all income.[86] However, at the same time, the largest source of revenue for a typical Catholic parish, the weekend offertory collection, is diminishing. Reports indicate that much of this reduction is due to the lack of trust as a result of the sexual abuse crises. At the same time, the cost of expenses related to investigating allegations, legal fees, and other costs has led to many dioceses and Catholic institutions filing for bankruptcy or taking other drastic fiscal measures, including selling property, liquidating assets, and often major salary cuts and reductions.[87]

Undoubtedly, these are challenging circumstances for all ecclesial leaders and tough decisions are necessary. However, the solution must be a collaborative effort by all ecclesial ministers, clergy and laity alike. Cardinal Joseph Tobin recently said, "A budget is a theological statement."[88] As parishes and diocese rely on lay ecclesial ministers to teach theology, celebrate the faith, and minister to the flock, these same ministers must be at the table as this "theological statement" is developed. By sharing the burdens of decision-making in terms of budget development, the gifts of lay ministers can also be instrumental in identifying solutions to budgetary challenges. In addition, these ministers often have the closest relationships with parishioners and can deliver the needed messages about parish stewardship regarding time, talent, and financial giving. Through these combined efforts we can truly "be stewards of the Church—collaborators and cooperators in continuing the redemptive work of Jesus Christ, which is the Church's essential mission."[89]

Clearly, the Church is coming to terms with what it means to have non-ordained ministers and the need to rely on those ministers for a large part of her apostolate. While acknowledging that "the Church's experience of lay participation in Christ's ministry is still maturing,"[90] the bishops have not taken steps to ensure that the dignity of work is upheld across its dioceses. Lay ecclesial ministers live in the liminal space between ordained ministry and what is often understood as the work of the laity. While the systems that govern priestly formation and governance have been developed and reworked over centuries, the systems for lay employees are nascent and often underdeveloped or completely absent. Moving away from at-will employment, ensuring pay equity, a commitment to family healthcare, educational investment, and including lay ecclesial minsters in the budgeting process are necessary steps that will reflect the covenant relationship between the employer Church and its employee ministers.

In the 1992 document *Stewardship: A Disciple's Response*, the U.S. bishops defined *stewards* as those who "receive God's gifts gratefully, cultivate them responsibly, share them lovingly in justice with others, and return them with increase to the Lord." Lay ecclesial ministers are a gift to the Church, both locally and universally. Pastors who view their lay ecclesial ministers through this lens of gift will acknowledge them through commissioning; nourish them through formation; share them with justice, by providing adequate remuneration and care for their families; and at some point, when blessing them to work in other vineyards, will do so confidently that they have increased in grace, faith, and hope in the Lord.

Chapter 6

THE WAY FORWARD

Our work as pastoral leaders is to create a work experience that feels like a healthy relationship for co-workers because when we do that, people start showing up more committed. Co-workers want to feel valued and appreciated, and cared for, and trusted, and included, and connected. As we move forward, we are defying the adage of shuffling deck chairs, or doing things the way we always have. We are not asking for equality among the ranks. We are calling for equity in our workplaces, regardless of gender, race, age, ability, color, national origin, religion, sexual orientation, or other differences. Leaders need to transcend their natural preferences when leading and developing people.

This book provides a mental model for a way forward, calling for leadership that respects and empowers the gifts of all, adaptability to respond to a diverse Church, having the resources for extraordinary work, providing backup for one another when there is a workload problem, and being a robust, thriving community of co-workers in the vineyard of the Lord.

Lee Shulman is an expert on professional continuing education. In his writing, he has emphasized that one of the marks of a profession is the way in which members of a profession attend to its development over time.[1] In some ways, this book seeks to be a resource for those concerned and committed to the overall development and health of ministry, especially lay ecclesial ministry. This last chapter, then, re-emphasizes what readers have learned here and how it can make a lasting difference in the ways they apply it. We bring to this work nearly twenty years of experience hosting conversations and theologically reflecting on the experiences of co-workers while advocating for a clearer recognition of the vocation of the laity. We understand, however, that the sustainability of any call for change and renewal rests with those most intimately connected to the challenge.

The infinite variety of human beings is what makes ministering so interesting, exciting, and challenging. It is also what makes it so difficult at times. Differences matter. Readers found that in the stories of our eight writers. They share the dilemmas that can emerge as committed, value-driven, and mission-focused people live out their vocational calls. For example, consider how the chaplain who is marginalized by her supervisor is different than the director of liturgy trying to deal with an excessive workload during peak liturgical seasons, or the pastoral leader terminated because of compromised values and unchallenged falsehoods. Looking at those stories from the outside, we might be surprised that the storyteller did not see the problem or challenge as clearly as we the reader. The fact is, the effort to understand how our identities are formed, how we expand our understanding by learning across our differences, and how there are concrete, specific ways to be enhance our interactions with others enables us to become observers in the midst of all our activity.

While there is a temptation to enshrine a single strategy that will work well with everybody, the truth is there needs to be several different strategies and tools available to us that we can use and adapt in a wide range of circumstances. The strategies and tools that we explored in this book included the following:

1. *To tell* the stories of lay ecclesial ministers: people's experience matters and from that experience we can gain insight into the challenges and opportunities to develop as ministers.

2. *To understand* the elements of a healthy workplace—community, control, fairness, financial well-being, reward, values, vocation, workload. There are concrete, specific areas of organizational life that can be shaped and enriched so that all benefit from a healthy work environment.

3. *To discover* individual identities and their influence on relationships across cultural differences so innovation and creativity flourish: "difference" as discussed here is an invitation to pay attention to the complexity of each person with whom we interact and with whom we strive to advance the mission of the gospel.

4. *To connect* a theology of covenant to a pastoral framework for ministerial relationships: the sort of culture change we advocate needs a sustaining source of inspiration to stay at the demanding work that change requires.

5. *To reframe* pastoral leadership in a hierarchical structure with an emphasis on inclusion, equity, diversity, justice, and cultural humility: this reframing is not original but flows from the wellsprings of the Church's own theological vision.

6. *To pivot* single story narratives to theologically reflect on our ministerial experiences as a way to discover God's action at the center of all ministry, whether individually, in small groups, or as a full staff, situating our experience within the broader story provided by Scripture and tradition enriches what we know, how we perceive, and where the next steps lie.

When we talk about sustaining a healthy ministerial workplace, we are talking about human sustainability—creating environments where people can thrive and experience physical and mental health and where our pastoral leaders do not face inevitable burnout or illness from institutional practices. In doing so they can focus their energies and creativity on the mission of the Church. Creating such environments is not pie-in-the-sky. While it might be tempting to let loose our inner cynic and snort at the prospect of real change, we bring this book to a close more convinced than ever that lay ecclesial ministers and clergy have the capacity for transformative action. The work is ours. No one will do it for us. We have the power to change our ministerial workplaces.

At the end of the final session of the 2020 conference, Professor C. Vanessa White from the Catholic Theological Union in Chicago gave participants a rousing missional charge. Her words capture the promising spirit of renewal we believe covenant holds out as we take up the challenge of creating and sustaining healthy workplaces.

> We have come together to celebrate, reflect, and pray on this journey of ministry as we call to mind what it means to be a lay ecclesial minister in today's environment. I am grateful to those who have framed this time in prayer and reflection. We have come together, even in this virtual realm, acknowledging the impact that pandemic, political divisiveness, and the

continued impact of racism evidenced in the ongoing protests against violence done to black, brown, and Asian bodies. We have come to affirm that we wish to create, sustain, and maintain healthy ministerial environments that are inclusive of all who work in the vineyard. We have come over these past few months to share our stories and to sing our songs and to proclaim the goodness and value of lay ministry. We have come to reflect on covenant-making, assessing where we are and where we are going and what we are creating.

What we focus on is what we give power to. The words of St. Paul have the power to guide and offer sustenance for the road ahead. I heard this text and in fact memorized it almost 30 years ago as a young adult Black Catholic Lay Woman starting off in professional ministry in the Church as the Director of the Claretian Volunteers and Lay Missionaries. At that time, while attending ministerial gatherings, I was overwhelmed and somewhat disheartened by the negative voices of others in ministry who were moving toward burnout and disillusionment in the Church. These words sustained me during difficult times in ministry, encouraged me in becoming my authentic self and so I invite you to again listen to the words of St. Paul as you get ready to go forth and do the work that God is calling of you.

In the presence of God and of Christ Jesus, I solemnly urge you to proclaim the message:

- Proclaim the message of what has taken place in the framework of these conversations.
- Proclaim the message that lay ministers and all who minister in the Church desire and need healthy and just workplaces.
- Proclaim the message that ongoing formation is expected within the traditional work week.
- Proclaim the message that we must be intentional about the inclusion of diverse work environments.

Be persistent whether the time is favorable or unfavorable.

The Way Forward

We live in a time that people do not want to be uncomfortable, do not want to be challenged to do what is right. But our God, that sweet Holy Spirit, calls us to be persistent, so at times we will need to convince, rebuke, and even encourage. That may mean speaking up about unjust hiring practices and conditions in ministerial settings or the lack of stipends—a just wage paid to ministers, including yourself. Sometimes we may feel like we are the lone voice but remember, as St. Paul reminds us, to be persistent and to be patient in our teaching. Laypeople know all about patience, sometimes you have to just breathe and then continue in the struggle.

For the time is coming
when people will not put up with sound doctrine,
but having itching ears, they will accumulate for themselves
teachers to suit their own desires.

- We have seen that in hiring practices in parishes and in dioceses persons are not always chosen because of their commitment to the mission of Jesus Christ or the people of God. Many times, the leadership is made of up those who surround themselves with those persons who will not challenge them. Be aware that you may even fall into the trap of being one of those teachers. This is where times of prayer, times of discernment, a good spiritual director, healthy bodily practices can assist in giving you the patience but also the discernment needed.

They will turn away from listening to the truth
and wander away to myths.

This is where a good sustaining community can be most helpful. Our partners in ministry are important in this journey. This time of pandemic has increased the sense of isolation as well as the proliferation of untruths found on the internet and in social media. We have to be persons of deep prayer, open to the Holy Spirit, humble of heart, and strong in spirit to turn away from these myths. Intentionally seeking a community that affirms the value of lay ecclesial ministry, of being a worker in the vineyard of the Lord can help remind us of why we went into ministry in the first place. A community is a reminder of the truth and the joy of lay ministry in the Church.

As for you, always be sober, endure suffering,
do the work of the evangelist,
carry out your ministry fully.

This is where a spirituality of resistance and resiliency is needed. We must resist that which turns us away from the Gospel of Jesus Christ, that weakens our resolve to be co-workers in the Vineyard of the Lord. Through prayer, shared story, and testimony and development of life-giving communities, we journey in hope, knowing that the road will not be easy nor the load always light. I am reminded of the words of a mentor, Fr. Chuck Faso—we are an Easter people and Alleluia is our Song. We must continue to have these crucial conversations about ministry—its challenges and its joys. We must continue to speak the truth to power—whoever that power is. We must acknowledge that there is a cross in our future, but sustained by that Sweet Holy Spirit, we are called to continue doing the work that God calls of us, to carry out your ministry—to fulfill your ministry with the Grace of God.

So, GO FORTH—DO THE WORK OF AN EVANGELIST—A DISCIPLE—FULFILL YOUR MINISTRY.

Appendix A
INDEX FOR HEALTHY MINISTERIAL WORKPLACES

This self-assessment tool is a resource for people as they reflect on the health of their workplaces using eight key elements. While there may be other elements, these eight represent key aspects of organizational life that impact people's attitudes, satisfaction, and engagement. For each element, there is a set of statements about practices known to positively affect that element. There may be other practices, but we have determined that these play a key role in workplace health.

The Index is for individual use and is a companion to the Healthy Ministerial Workplace Covenant Assessment. The latter is for a workplace group to use as a reflection guide in examining the health of their workplace and, more important, designing specific, concrete actions to improve and strengthen their relationships and the workplace. In completing the Index, people should select the assessment category that most accurately reflects their experience. Avoid the extremes of rating everything high because "that's what good people do" or rating everything low because you are annoyed that more is not being done or being done better.

The results of the Index can serve as a reflective resource as individuals consider how the results might be impacting their lives and performance as ministers in the workplace. Having five or more elements scored at 4 or 5 indicate a level of engagement in the workplace suggesting health. Having five or more elements scored at 1, 2, or 3 might show a movement toward disengagement. Disengagement that is ignored contributes to eventual burnout.

Neither the Index nor the summary graph are predicative. They are designed to provide a more structured way for thinking about workplace health and to encourage reflection.

For each of the following indicators, select one of the following response categories that best reflects your judgment based on your experience and perceptions:

ELEMENT: VOCATION					
Practices	Strongly Agree	Agree	Neither Agree nor Disagree	Disagree	Strongly Disagree
1. Workplace leadership actively recognizes what I do as a ministerial vocation.	5	4	3	2	1
2. I continue to feel called by God and the community to the work with which I am entrusted.	5	4	3	2	1
3. My position calls me to use my greatest gifts and skills to serve the people of God.	5	4	3	2	1
4. My workplace and those I serve support and affirm me as a person in my ministerial vocation.	5	4	3	2	1
5. I am open to new movements of the Spirit in my vocation.	5	4	3	2	1

ELEMENT: VALUES					
Practices	Strongly Agree	Agree	Neither Agree nor Disagree	Disagree	Strongly Disagree
1. The values that guide my practice of ministry align with the stated values we profess in our workplace.	5	4	3	2	1

Appendix A: Index for Healthy Ministerial Workplaces

2. I integrate the stated values of our workplace in my daily ministry.	5	4	3	2	1
3. Scripture and theology form and inform the way I minister.	5	4	3	2	1
4. I am able to receive feedback when the way I minister does not align with workplace values.	5	4	3	2	1
5. I feel safe giving feedback when actions or decisions do not align with workplace values.	5	4	3	2	1

ELEMENT: WORKLOAD					
Practices	Strongly Agree	Agree	Neither Agree nor Disagree	Disagree	Strongly Disagree
1. My workload is reasonable, enabling me to meet the expectations for my position.	5	4	3	2	1
2. My responsibilities in my ministry are commensurate with my skills and credentials.	5	4	3	2	1
3. My workload is outlined in a clearly stated job/role description.	5	4	3	2	1
4. My workload enables me to set appropriate boundaries around my time and priorities.	5	4	3	2	1
5. I have sufficient opportunities annually for personal and professional development that my ministry site actively supports.	5	4	3	2	1

ELEMENT: FINANCIAL WELL-BEING

Practices	Strongly Agree	Agree	Neither Agree nor Disagree	Disagree	Strongly Disagree
1. I have adequate financial resources to fulfill the vision of the ministry.	5	4	3	2	1
2. I am aware the salary for my position is a just and competitive salary.	5	4	3	2	1
3. I have adequate training to manage my budgetary responsibilities for my ministry.	5	4	3	2	1
4. The budgeting process is clear and provides opportunities for input.	5	4	3	2	1
5. My benefits package is wholistic, including provisions for ongoing professional and spiritual growth.	5	4	3	2	1
6. I am able to provide decently for my own needs and those of my family.	5	4	3	2	1

ELEMENT: FAIRNESS

Practices	Strongly Agree	Agree	Neither Agree nor Disagree	Disagree	Strongly Disagree
1. Our processes and policies are fair to all employees and volunteers.	5	4	3	2	1
2. I contribute to shaping expectations and assumptions about how work gets done.	5	4	3	2	1
3. The annual review process contributes positively to my ongoing development.	5	4	3	2	1

Appendix A: Index for Healthy Ministerial Workplaces

4. I am equipped to recruit, select, form, and evaluate volunteers.	5	4	3	2	1
5. My workplace operates in a way that does not discriminate by race, ethnicity, national origin, gender, sexual orientation, disability, and language preferences.	5	4	3	2	1

ELEMENT: COMMUNITY					
Practices	Strongly Agree	Agree	Neither Agree nor Disagree	Disagree	Strongly Disagree
1. Open and honest communication among the staff supports and encourages me.	5	4	3	2	1
2. I work at building trust with my colleagues for effective teamwork.	5	4	3	2	1
3. I value individual differences in the workplace and take action to make all feel welcome and accepted.	5	4	3	2	1
4. My workplace provides opportunities for community building that supports collaboration and a positive spirit among us.	5	4	3	2	1
5. Our regular opportunities as staff for prayer and faith-sharing ground my ministry.	5	4	3	2	1
6. I strive to cooperate with others to create and sustain a healthy workplace.	5	4	3	2	1

SUSTAINING A HEALTHY MINISTERIAL WORKPLACE

ELEMENT: CONTROL					
Practices	Strongly Agree	Agree	Neither Agree nor Disagree	Disagree	Strongly Disagree
1. I generally have adequate control over my time and resources to accomplish what is expected.	5	4	3	2	1
2. I have sufficient freedom and authority to make decisions based on the responsibilities of my job description.	5	4	3	2	1
3. Our patterns of cooperation as a team are effective and integrated.	5	4	3	2	1
4. I am able to use processes already in place to resolve conflicts and concerns.	5	4	3	2	1
5. I have enough discretion in my work to exercise innovation and creativity in the face of emerging changes in ministry.	5	4	3	2	1

ELEMENT: REWARD					
Practices	Strongly Agree	Agree	Neither Agree nor Disagree	Disagree	Strongly Disagree
1. My ministry offers me a sense of personal and professional satisfaction.	5	4	3	2	1
2. I am given opportunities to discern how to develop and apply my gifts in new, life-giving ways.	5	4	3	2	1
3. Due to the complexity of my position, I have flexibility in scheduling, prioritizing assignments, and collaborating with others.	5	4	3	2	1

Appendix A: Index for Healthy Ministerial Workplaces

4. My supervisor and colleagues recognize my contributions to our common work.	5	4	3	2	1
5. I feel appreciated.	5	4	3	2	1
6. In peak cycles, I can depend on others to assist.	5	4	3	2	1

Appendix B
REFLECTION GUIDE
A Covenant-Based Ministry

The focus on building and sustaining healthy ministerial workplaces pivots on the degree staff members can commit themselves to work together in a spirit of covenant (see chapter 2). Before completing the following Index, we recommend that the staff meet for an hour to reflect on the statement of covenant we have presented. The purpose of this reflection is to orient staff members to a new way of interacting that flows from their deepest values and sustains the normal ups and downs of practicing new skills.

The session might best begin by using a *lectio* format. After a first reading of the covenant, ask people to identify a phrase or idea that stands out for them. Offer them to the whole group one by one. Then after a second reading, people identify what might be unclear or puzzling. Depending on the size of the group, have them discuss their observations in pairs or groups of three, reporting a summary to the whole group. Finally, after a third reading of the covenant, ask people for ideas about how wording might be changed or adapted to better reflect the spirit of the group. Collect suggestions and ask for a couple of volunteers to work with the suggestions and craft a revised covenant statement.

A statement is an inert document unless it becomes an active part of a group's life. Whether a staff adopts the covenant we have framed or creates a revision of its own, it needs to be revisited frequently. It might be part of the opening prayer for staff meetings or for professional development sessions we describe in other resources in this section of the book. When conflict arises, the covenant should be the basis on which it is resolved in terms of how people reach some sort of mutual understanding. Parish committees or councils need to be aware of the covenant and explore how members of committees conduct their work.

In the end, a covenant is a public statement, not a private agreement. It is a commitment to act in ways that build up, enrich, and bring energy to group life. It is not magical, but it can be powerful in making workplaces healthier by galvanizing people's attention and action. This is what changes a culture.

STATEMENT OF WORKPLACE COVENANT
A vocation to pastoral ministry is a call to advance the mission of the gospel. The work we share finds expression in evangelization and catechesis, worship, pastoral care, outreach, community building, stewardship, and leadership. Our success is measured by the growth in knowledge of God, co-responsibility for the reign of God, and spirit of hope we cultivate in those to whom we minister and in ourselves. Ours is collaborative work, as clergy and lay ecclesial ministers. We form a community of ministerial leaders bound together by a commitment to Christ, his gospel, and the care of God's people. We will risk being transformed. We recognize that creating a healthy ministerial workplace is a responsibility each of us shares.

HOW TO USE THIS INDEX

1. Each staff or team member should complete the Index and use it as an opportunity to look at their workplace in two ways. The first is to be as objective as possible. That's why the Index asks for concrete examples of how each element is working or not working. The second opportunity is to begin the process of considering how working toward covenant relationships would contribute to how this element is managed. Responses should reflect individuals' best judgment.

2. Someone from the staff should be chosen to compile the results and prepare a summary of scores *and* examples given by respondents. Staff members should submit their responses anonymously.

3. The results should be sent to every staff member prior to the group's meeting at least a week in advance. Staff members should read the results carefully and make note of any questions or observations that arise.

4. When the group meets to discuss the results, the stated purpose is to deepen an understanding of the strengths and challenges in the organization and their impact on the health of the workplace.

5. A facilitator should be chosen whose primary responsibility is to deal with the process of the discussion; this will limit her or his ability to be an active participant in the discussion (see the introduction to this section of the book). Someone should volunteer to take notes so that good ideas and important points do not get lost.

6. At the start of the session, the facilitator reads aloud the statement of covenant and repeats the purpose for gathering. The facilitator also asks what sort of guidelines would be most helpful to ensure a productive, positive conversation in which all feel welcome. On a large newsprint easel pad, write the suggestions down for all to see and ask people to agree to observe them during the session.

7. The facilitator begins by asking staff members, based on their reading of the results, which principles seem to be the strongest within their workplace and which seem to pose the most challenge. The facilitator helps the group reach shared understanding although there may be instances in which there is a clear split in perceptions within the staff. Acknowledge these by putting a star after each of them.

8. Then the facilitator indicates that the group will use an appreciative inquiry process to build on those principles that the group generally assesses positively—*they describe us most of the time*. This encourages the group to work from its strengths. Begin by asking people to recall specific examples that explain why these principles are an active part of the group's life. Build a list of examples on the pad.

Appendix B: Reflection Guide

9. The facilitator points out that the group is already practicing covenant in some specific ways and that it is with this in mind that attention now turns to those principles that need development. After highlighting the principles needing development (for example, *this describes us a little* or *this needs development*), ask the group to quietly reflect on ways they can leverage their strengths and current practices to improve or deepen those principles in the workplace. After a few minutes, provide three sticky dots for participants to select the three examples they believe will help them take effect.

10. Create an action plan and schedule for implementing actions that will make a difference, strengthen covenant, and be sustained over time.

COVENANT-BASED REFLECTION GUIDE FOR MINISTERIAL WORKPLACES

Creating and sustaining a healthy ministerial workplace is both a theological and practical task. It is theological because is calls for alignment of core gospel values and workplace practices. At the same time, there are practical actions needed so that our aspirations to live in covenant relationships transform what we do each day. This reflective assessment bridges the distance between aspiration and action and seeks to foster deep, honest reflection as a work group seeks to improve the health of its workplace.

1. We share a conviction that the sacraments of initiation form the common basis for our shared participation in the threefold ministry of Christ, who is priest, prophet, and king. We also acknowledge the complementarity of our distinct vocations as ordained and lay ecclesial ministers.

1	2	3	4	5	6	7	8	9	10
This describes us most of the time.					This does not describe us most of the time.				
How are we incorporating this practice already?										
What seems to get in the way of living out this purpose?										

2. We gather for prayer, community, and learning, knowing that the inspiration of the Scriptures and theological reflection on our ministerial practice ground us in sustaining right relationships and a healthy ministerial workplace.

1	2	3	4	5	6	7	8	9	10
This describes us most of the time.					**This does not describe us most of the time.**				
How are we incorporating this practice already?									
What seems to get in the way of living out this purpose?									

3. Our mission and vision provide the values we seek to embody in every aspect of our work and that those shared values are a primary source of mutual good as we evaluate our ministerial leadership.

1	2	3	4	5	6	7	8	9	10
This describes us most of the time.					**This does not describe us most of the time.**				
How are we incorporating this practice already?									
What seems to get in the way of living out this purpose?									

4. We strive to deepen the human competencies needed for effective teamwork and ministerial leadership. These include skills for strong interpersonal communication, intercultural competence, decision-making, management of conflict, ways to process difficult issues, and sustained collaboration across our designated positions.

1	2	3	4	5	6	7	8	9	10
This describes us most of the time.					**This does not describe us most of the time.**				
How are we incorporating this practice already?									
What seems to get in the way of living out this purpose?									

Appendix B: Reflection Guide

5. We mutually define a manageable workload that provides the opportunity to serve the needs of the community through one's designated ministry as well as one's charisms and deep passions, to pursue career objectives, and to develop professionally.

1	2	3	4	5	6	7	8	9	10
This describes us most of the time.					**This does not describe us most of the time.**				
How are we incorporating this practice already?										
What seems to get in the way of living out this purpose?										

6. We have in place a regular system of evaluation that provides insight into our work performance, raising up our accomplishments and finding resources and ways to address areas of needed growth.

1	2	3	4	5	6	7	8	9	10
This describes us most of the time.					**This does not describe us most of the time.**				
How are we incorporating this practice already?										
What seems to get in the way of living out this purpose?										

7. To be in right relationship with all employees and volunteers, we practice being open to receiving and giving skilled and compassionate feedback.

1	2	3	4	5	6	7	8	9	10
This describes us most of the time.					**This does not describe us most of the time.**				
How are we incorporating this practice already?										
What seems to get in the way of living out this purpose?										

SUSTAINING A HEALTHY MINISTERIAL WORKPLACE

8. We interact out of a shared understanding that the quality and effectiveness of our professional relationships have significant impact on those to whom and with whom we minister.

1	2	3	4	5	6	7	8	9	10
This describes us most of the time.					**This does not describe us most of the time.**				
How are we incorporating this practice already?									
What seems to get in the way of living out this purpose?									

9. We contribute to developing and sustaining a healthy workplace by individual and team ongoing education, ministerial formation, and the cultivation of imagination and creativity in whatever forms they might take.

1	2	3	4	5	6	7	8	9	10
This describes us most of the time.					**This does not describe us most of the time.**				
How are we incorporating this practice already?									
What seems to get in the way of living out this purpose?									

10. We work at creating inclusive communities in which we cultivate respect for diversity of cultural traditions, languages, theological visions, and devotional and spiritual practices.

1	2	3	4	5	6	7	8	9	10
This describes us most of the time.					**This does not describe us most of the time.**				
How are we incorporating this practice already?									
What seems to get in the way of living out this purpose?									

Appendix B: Reflection Guide

11. We provide in a fair and transparent manner for the just and financial well-being of all employees.

1	2	3	4	5	6	7	8	9	10
This describes us most of the time.					**This does not describe us most of the time.**				
How are we incorporating this practice already?									
What seems to get in the way of living out this purpose?									

12. We abide in the covenant through the principle of subsidiarity, when those closest to a problem or pastoral concern will be consulted for deeper understanding.

1	2	3	4	5	6	7	8	9	10
This describes us most of the time.					**This does not describe us most of the time.**				
How are we incorporating this practice already?									
What seems to get in the way of living out this purpose?									

Appendix C

LEARNING FROM OUR STORIES

Principles for Productive Discussions

Several years ago, a parish pastoral council was in chaos. If anything could go wrong, it did. Council members were at odds with each other, staff was in disarray, and the mission was out of focus. During one contentious council meeting, a member finally said in exasperation, "You know, we are far better at describing a problem than ever doing anything real about it." So many organizational conversations follow that path of exacting description and no real action. Over the past few years, we have learned a great deal about what is necessary to create and sustain a healthy ministerial workplace. As we share that insight in this book, however, we are aware that the work of our contributors, the participants in our online Co-workers Vineyard of the Lord Conference, and six months of crucial conversations about the workplace may all end up being just one more elaborate description of the problem.

Our intent from the beginning has been to stimulate sustained conversation focused on both naming the reality of ministerial workplaces and creating action responses that make a difference—that change the culture. We gather these resources under the banner "We Are the Ones We Have Been Waiting For." This phrase was first introduced by Jamaican American activist, teacher, and poet June Jordan in her poem "For Women in South Africa" (1978) and again in a letter written by the Elders of the Hopi Nation of Oraibi, Arizona (2000).

Based on Jordan's earlier work, her poem inspires hope and long vision. The same Spirit remains steadfast today for the ministerial work of lay ecclesial ministers. It captures our purpose: waiting for someone else to do what is needed, waiting until the structures of Church life are perfect, waiting until bishops and clergy are in full agreement about co-workers in the vineyard of the Lord—all are futile. All pastoral ministers need to be diligent in gaining deeper self-understanding, so they recognize their differences, the differences in others, and the ways we are able to work effectively and missionally across those differences. This was the focus of chapter 3. They need a clear-eyed understanding of the strengths as well as challenges in their workplaces. Too often, we think we know what's going on when in fact we have cobbled together bits of data, all of which may be accurate, but which are incomplete. That is why we developed the Covenant Index found in appendix B. We know that we are at our best when we work from our strengths to address our shortcomings. The Index is a tool that gives us a full picture of the situation.

With these resources, we present discussion models aimed at supporting ministry staffs to be their own agents of change. The models draw on the material presented in this book as a way to advance the principle that change happens when understanding *and* commitment come together. These are activities that contribute to ongoing professional development critical for building and sustaining a healthy workplace.

THE RESPONSIBILITY FOR PROFESSIONAL DEVELOPMENT

Lee Shulman has researched and written about the nature of professions. One of his conclusions, shared widely, is that a profession is based on a clear body of knowledge, tested principles of practice, and ethical standards.[1] He has also noted that those who think of themselves as professional have a responsibility to continue their own growth in knowledge and skill while attending to the well-being of the profession itself. There are many of us in universities and schools of theology who can offer advice and insight about pastoral ministry and pastoral leadership. We are colleagues and companions to this important work. But what actually happens "in the trenches" is beyond our research and scholarship. We rely on you—can only rely on you—to adapt and implement what we see to what is best known and do firsthand.

Professional development has two primary focal points. The first is deepening the knowledge base that informs and guides professional practice. The formal study of theology and Scripture begun in graduate school become active parts of one's thinking and doing in ministry. Similarly, continuous learning around the pastoral arts—teaching, counseling, ritualization, communication, evangelization, and so on—keep pastoral ministers alert to how they might enhance what they practice. The second focus in professional development is gaining insight into how one responds to the wide range of interactions that occur, deepening a sense of God's presence and action in one's life, learning how to integrate the factors that form one's identity as a person and as a minister, so they become assets rather than obstacles to effective professional practice.

The models for professional development we offer in all of these resources assume group work. This does not diminish the importance of what one does as an individual. Rather, we find that developing a healthy workplace is something that those who comprise that workplace best do together. These models encourage well-structured conversations with appropriate boundaries that invite all perspectives to see the whole context. How I might as an individual see and define the issues and challenges we have, while important, is not definitive. Being able to hear and understand multiple perspectives—especially when some don't agree with mine—expands the vision of where effective, positive action lies.

CONVENING A PRODUCTIVE CONVERSATION: GENERAL PRINCIPLES

In her book *The Art of Gathering*, Priya Parker says that all productive conversations rest on two key principles: a clear purpose and rules of engagement.[2] Having a clear purpose guides a conversation through the thicket of ideas and questions that typically arise. A clear purpose names what will be included and what will not. At the start of a session, it is good practice to write the purpose of the discussion on a newsprint pad as a reminder to all present. This becomes critical to avoid sessions that subtlety are designed to "fix" someone or that wander into a universe of issues with no roadmap in sight. Stated purposes set boundaries such as we are here today to explore fairness and equity of our current policies and procedures and to recommend specific changes we believe are essential.

Having some stated rules of engagement, or norms, shapes productive conversations. Naming and monitoring those norms ultimately help people do their best work together. One way to do this is to ask each member of the group to identify one rule or norm that helps them participate fully in a discussion. Another option is to offer a set of norms that address key aspects of discussions. Here are six we have field tested numerous times:

Be present. This is an invitation to silence phones, but it is also a request that people strive to be present mentally to what is happening—not what they wish would be happening.

Practice hospitality. Because people participate differently, creating the space for people to engage at their own pace is important. Hospitality means actively making people feel welcome to engage in the group.

Listen. Listening is the gateway to tapping into the wisdom of the group. It involves paying attention to what is being said, seeking clarity to understand what is being said, and acknowledging what someone is offering to the group.

Speak. The bookend for listening is speaking. While it is fine as an introvert to take time to frame what one wants to say, being silent and seldom offering one's insights, asking questions, or providing information does not fulfill the responsibility one has a member of the group.

Be curious. Curiosity is a behavior that reminds us we are on a journey of discovery. When someone asks a question or makes a statement, we should be curious about what they mean versus what we *think* they mean. Being curious is also one of the ways we manage conflict. When someone expresses an opinion that is contrary to ours, we can choose to argue how they are wrong, or we can probe what they mean.

Trust the process, believe in the outcome. Undertaking something in good faith offers a way to span imperfections that arise. It is an invitation to assume that the purposes of the workshop are important, and the Spirit works within us toward a positive outcome.

However, you generate or state the rules of engagement, be clear how important it is for each person to commit to observe them for the good of the group's work.

ANCHORED IN PRAYER

Discussions about ministerial life need to flow from prayer. It is the language that keeps us grounded in our ideals and beliefs. While groups are fully capable of determining what form of prayer best works for them, we emphasize that any session designed for professional development of pastoral ministers must anchor itself in prayer. In our own experience, the quality of conversation and the capacity to move to a productive conclusion increase notably as a result of dwelling in the core values and beliefs that form the heart of discipleship.

FOCUSED ON ACTION

People grow weary of "one more damn meeting" when most conversations end up with no clear idea of the next step forward. Not only are the next steps part of the purpose statement, but a process needs to be in place to ensure those steps are taken. This include a timeline, people with responsibility for certain things, and the way the group will know the steps have been taken and the results. This moves from "wishing we could get this done" to "here is what we will do."

COMMITTED TO EFFECTIVE COMMUNICATION AND MUTUAL TRUST

Productive discussions focused on professional development need to have everyone in the room and fully participative. Being in the room, of course, has nothing to do with physical presence. We have all taken our bodies to meetings but were mentally and emotionally elsewhere. Part of being present is believing that I will be heard, that what I have to say matters. It also means that I will strive to listen to others to understand what they are really saying, not what I assume they mean. Moreover, I will actively respect the ideas of others even when I do not fully agree with them. Because we are all very able to converse, we may conclude too readily that we are effective communicators. That is a dangerous assumption. Every time a group meets, especially a long-standing group, the members need to recommit themselves to listen to understand and to speak to be understood. Underlying effective communication is the bonding power of trust. Without trust, every discussion ends up being a presentation of opinions. I speak, she speaks, he speaks. Nothing much new is said much less learned, and action is as possible as riding a unicorn. We have worked with staffs where trust was absent or hanging on by a thread. Not only does this corrupt a workplace, but it also makes change nearly impossible. Trust emerges through effective communication, building relationships that are robust, and seeking and extending forgiveness. In every staff mistakes will be made. We will be misunderstood, will misunderstand, will misspeak, or break a commitment. Too often, we gloss over these happenings too quickly or assume a colleague "knows I didn't mean it." Ministry is demanding interpersonal work with those to whom we minister and with those with whom we minister as a staff. Forgiveness as an active practice keeps us attuned to one another so that a mistake does not become a barrier to trust.

DESIGN AN ORDERED CONVERSATION

There is a misconception that good conversations are free-form and spontaneous. Good order is not meant to be a corset, controlling what happens as a group convenes. Commonsense practices like having a general outline of the process and expectations create a common playing field. Providing a timeframe and respecting it encourages everyone to make the best use of the time allotted to meet the session's purpose. Have a facilitator and empower her or him to figuratively "rule with an iron fist." A good facilitator is charged with paying attention to the dynamics of the group. They ensure that what people are saying is heard. They take note of who has not had a chance to contribute and invite them into the circle, or they may need to encourage someone who contributes too much to make space for others. The facilitator summarizes the discussion at various points to help the group assess where it is and reminds the group where it is on the agenda. Facilitators from outside the staff can be helpful but may be a luxury. However, facilitators who are also members of the staff need to accept that their role is to deal with the group's process and limit their active participation. Finally, it is important to have someone take notes and watch the clock. The notes need not be elaborate, but a record of a discussion is invaluable for harvesting good ideas, important questions, and action steps, and those responsible for them. Discussions are important forums for accomplishing the inner work of ministry service. Good order simply makes that work more effective and ultimately more efficient.

Appendix D

USING THE NARRATIVES AND THEOLOGICAL REFLECTIONS FOR ONGOING FORMATION

The steps that follow provide a model for using the narratives and theological reflections in this book (chapters 1 and 6) as part of an ongoing formation event. Ministry teams should adapt the model in light of their circumstances and needs.

1. Select a narrative linked to an element of a healthy ministerial workplace that has some urgency for participants: community, control, fairness, reward, workload, values, financial well-being, or vocation.

2. In addition to providing time for shared prayer, keep in mind the principles for a productive conversation in appendix C.

3. Have someone read the selected narrative aloud. This gives it a common voice and sharpens attention to its details.

4. After the reading, provide a brief period of quiet time for participants to reflect on the discussion questions:

    - With whom or what do you identify in this narrative?
    - What biases are evident?
    - How are power differences present?
    - How would you respond differently?

5. Next, divide the group into smaller discussion teams (2–4 people each). Team members take turns sharing their responses, and the team prepares a brief summary of their primary observations about the narrative.

6. There are two possible approaches to presenting the theological reflection associated with the selected narrative: (a) Provide five to ten minutes for people to read the reflection individually and underline ideas they find significant or that raise questions. (b) Have several people take turns reading the theological reflection aloud, paragraph by paragraph. Once again, this is a way to catch tone, emotions, and emphases that might get lost by reading it silently.

7. After the reading, ask participants to spend a few quiet minutes individually thinking about these discussion questions:

   - How does theological reflection shift the original narrative for you?
   - What are the implications of this theological reflection for ministerial identity?
   - What is the impact of this theological reflection on the practice of ministry?

8. Next, send participants back into their teams to explore the discussion teams.

9. In a plenary session, invite participants to share their ideas about the following:

How could what we did today advance our effort to sustain a covenant-based ministry?

NOTES

CHAPTER 1: STORIES FROM THE VINEYARD

1. Katlin B. Curtice, *Native, Identity, Belonging, and Rediscovering God* (Grand Rapids, MI: Brazos, 2020), 5.

CHAPTER 2: FROM FIELD HOSPITAL TO THRIVING VINEYARD

1. Saint John's School of Theology and Seminary, National Symposium on Lay Ecclesial Ministry, 2007, https://www.csbsju.edu/sot/sem/lifelong-learning/lay-ecclesial-ministry/2007-national-symposium-on-lay-ecclesial-ministry.

2. "Toward Canonical Consideration of the Authorization of Lay Ecclesial Ministers for Ministry," Saint John's School of Theology and Seminary, 2015, https://www.csbsju.edu/lemsymposium.

3. "The Church as a Field Hospital: Caring for Our Own; A Position Paper of the National Association for Lay Ministry to Our Bishops and Those Tasked with Carrying Out Their Directives," National Association for Lay Ecclesial Ministry, 2022.

4. Teresa Watanabe, "A Divine View of Van Gogh," *Los Angeles Times*, January 23, 1999, https://www.latimes.com/archives/la-xpm-1999-jan-23-me-835-story.html.

5. *Evangelii Gaudium* 85.

6. Jeffrey Pfeffer, *Dying for a Paycheck: How Modern Management Harms Employee Health and Company Performance—and What We Can Do about It* (New York: Harper-Collins, 2018).

7. Angie Hong, "Women of Color in Ministry Are Not Scarce, Just Unsupported," Bearings Online, Feb. 3, 2022, https://collegevilleinstitute

.org/bearings/women-of-color-in-ministry-are-not-scarce-just-unsupported/.

8. Brian McLaren, *Finding Our Way Again: The Return of the Ancient Practices* (Nashville: Thomas Nelson, 2008), 126–28.

9. Parker Palmer, "Leading from Within," in *Let Your Life Speak: Listening for the Voice of Vocation* (Hoboken, NJ: Wiley, 2000), 3.

10. Christina Maslach, *The Cost of Caring* (Los Altos, CA: Malor Books, 2015), 2.

11. Maslach, *The Cost of Caring*, 3–6.

12. Maslach, *The Cost of Caring*, 1–23.

13. Michael P. Leiter and Christina Maslach, *Banish Burnout: Six Strategies for Improving Your Relationship with Work* (San Francisco: Wiley, 2005), 109–28.

14. Leiter and Maslach, *Banish Burnout*, 71–90.

15. Leiter and Maslach, *Banish Burnout*, 129–48.

16. Leiter and Maslach, *Banish Burnout*, 91–108.

17. Leiter and Maslach, *Banish Burnout*, 49–70.

18. Leiter and Maslach, *Banish Burnout*, 149–66.

19. Peter Block, *Community: The Structure of Belonging* (San Francisco: Berret-Koehler, 2008), 9–10.

20. C. Horwitz, *The Love That Does Justice: Spiritual Activism in Dialogue with Social Justices*, ed. M. A. Edwards and S. G. Post (Stony Brook, NY: Unlimited Love Press), 53–56.

CHAPTER 3: BEYOND THE SINGLE STORY

1. Chimamanda Ngozi Adichie, "The Danger of a Single Story," August 7, 2016, TED talk, https://www.ted.com/talks/chimamanda_ngozi_adichie_the_danger_of_a_single_story.

2. C. Kluckhohn and A. L. Kroeber, eds., *Culture* (New York: Random House, 1952), 181.

3. Geert Hofstede et al., *Cultures and Organizations: Software of the Mind* (New York: McGraw Hill, 1997), 5.

4. Edgar Schein, *Organizational Culture and Leadership* (San Francisco: Jossey-Bass, 2004), 17.

5. Edward T. Hall, *The Hidden Dimension* (New York: Anchor Books, 1969).

6. See David A. Livermore, *Cultural Intelligence: Improving Your CQ to Engage Our Multicultural World* (Grand Rapids: Baker Academic,

Notes

2009), 79–91, for a much fuller treatment of the iceberg theory and how it helps one get below the surface of relationship dynamics.

7. Livermore, *Cultural Intelligence*, 188.

8. This section draws on the research of Hofstede et al., *Cultures and Organizations*; Livermore, *Cultural Intelligence*; and Tara Harvey's course, "Intercultural Learning," True North Intercultural, 2020.

9. Livermore, *Cultural Intelligence*, 123–27.

10. Livermore, *Cultural Intelligence*, 128–29.

11. Livermore, *Cultural Intelligence*, 130–32.

12. Livermore, *Cultural Intelligence*, 132–35.

13. Livermore, *Cultural Intelligence*, 138.

14. Livermore, *Cultural Intelligence*, 135–37.

15. Gert Jan Hofstede et al., *Exploring Culture: Exercises, Stories and Synthetic Cultures* (Yarmouth, ME: Intercultural Press, 2002), 42.

16. Hofstede et al., *Cultures and Organizations*, 120–21.

17. Hofstede et al., *Cultures and Organizations*, 89–90.

18. Kelly Hannum et al., eds., *Leading across Differences* (San Francisco: Wiley, 2010).

19. Hannum et al., *Leading across Differences*, 11.

20. Hannum et al., *Leading across Differences*, 236.

21. Hannum et al., *Leading across Differences*, 13.

22. Hannum et al., *Leading across Differences*, 14.

23. Hannum et al., *Leading across Differences*, 14.

24. Katherine A. Yeager and Susan Bauer-Wu, "Cultural Humility: Essential Foundation for Clinical Researchers," *Applied Nursing Research* 26, no. 4 (Nov 2013): 251–56, https://pubmed.ncbi.nlm.nih.gov/23938129/.

25. Marti R. Jewell and Mark Mogilka, "'Open Wide the Doors to Christ': A Study of Catholic Social Innovation for Parish Vitality" (Fadica, 2020), https://www.hiltonfoundation.org/wp-content/uploads/2020/08/Open-Wide-the-Doors-to-Christ—A-Study-of-Catholic-Social-Innovation-for-Parish-Vitality-Executive-Summary.pdf.

26. Jewell and Mogilka, "Open Wide the Doors."

27. United States Bishop Conference (USCCB), "U.S. National Synthesis 2021–2023," https://www.usccb.org/resources/us-national-synthesis-2021-2023-synod.

28. USCCB, "U.S. National Synthesis 2021–2023."

29. USCCB, "U.S. National Synthesis 2021–2023."

30. USCCB, "U.S. National Synthesis 2021–2023."

31. USCCB, "U.S. National Synthesis 2021–2023."
32. USCCB, "U.S. National Synthesis 2021–2023."
33. Hannum et al., *Leading across Differences*, 194.
34. Hannum et al., *Leading across Differences*, 195.
35. Hannum et al., *Leading across Differences*, 195.
36. Hannum et al., *Leading across Differences*, 195.
37. Hannum et al., *Leading across Differences*, 195.
38. U.S. Census Bureau, "Year of Birth by Current Marital Status, Whether First Marriage Ended, Number of Times, Race, and Sex for Person Born between 1900 and 1954" (June 1971), https://www2.census.gov/programs-surveys/demo/tables/marriage-and-divorce/1971/p20-239-1972-t1.pdf.
39. U.S. Census Bureau, "Currently Divorced People as a Percent of People Who Have Ever Been Married" (USAFacts, 2022), https://usafacts.org/data/topics/people-society/population-and-demographics/population-data/net-divorce-rate-currently-divorced-as-of-ever-married/.
40. "Study: Divorce Is Up Significantly in Vietnam," *Saigoneer*, August 27, 2014, https://saigoneer.com/vietnam-news/2592-study-divorce-is-up-significantly-in-vietnam.
41. Jennifer Brown, *How to Be an Inclusive Leader: Your Role in Creating Cultures of Belonging Where Everyone Can Thrive* (Oakland, CA: Barrett-Koehler, 2019), 4.
42. B. M. Ferdman et al., "Inclusive Behavior and the Experience of Inclusion," in *What Makes an Organization Inclusive: Measures, HR, Practices and Climate*, ed. B. G. Chung (symposium presented at the Annual Meeting of the Academy of Management, Chicago, August 2009).
43. Joan Chittister, *The Monastic Heart: 50 Simple Practices for a Contemplative and Fulfilling Life* (New York: Convergent, 2021), 13.
44. Chittister, *The Monastic Heart*, 10.
45. Andrew B. Newberg and Mark Robert Waldman, *How God Changes Your Brain: Breakthrough Findings from a Leading Neuroscientist* (New York: Ballentine Books, 2009), 104.
46. Bryan Spoon, *Neuroscience and the Fruit of the Spirit* (Glendale: WI: Talk Publishing, 2020), 15.
47. Spoon, *Neuroscience and the Fruit of the Spirit*, 45.
48. Deloitte and Victorian Equal Opportunity and Human Rights Commission, *Waiter, Is That Inclusion in My Soup? A New Recipe to Improve Business Performance* (May 2013), https://www2.deloitte.com/

content/dam/Deloitte/au/Documents/human-capital/deloitte-au-hc-diversity-inclusion-soup-0513.pdf?bingParse.

CHAPTER 4: CALLED TO BE EXTRAORDINARY

1. Frederick Buechner, *Wishful Thinking: A Seeker's ABC* (New York: HarperOne, 1993), 118–19.

2. M. S. West et al., "Collective Leadership for Cultures of High-Quality Healthcare," *Journal of Organizational Effectiveness: People and Performance* 1, no. 3 (2014): 240–260.

3. Sherwood G. Lingenfelter, *Leading Cross Culturally: Covenant Relationships for Effective Christian Leadership* (Grand Rapids, MI: Baker Academic, 2008), 80.

4. Richard M. Gula, *Just Ministry: Professional Ethics for Pastoral Ministers* (Mahwah, NJ: Paulist Press, 2010).

5. Gretchen Ki Steidle, *Leading from Within: Conscious Social Change and Mindfulness for Social Innovation* (Cambridge, MA: MIT Press, 2018), 106.

6. Jennifer Brown, *How to Be an Inclusive Leader: Your Role in Creating Cultures of Belonging Where Everyone Can Thrive*, 2nd ed. (Oakland, CA: Berrett-Koehler, 2022), 102.

7. Arthur E. Zannoni, "The Biblical Covenant: Bonding with God," presentation notes shared with the authors.

8. Zannoni, "The Biblical Covenant."

9. W. Brueggemann, "Covenant as a Subversive Paradigm," *The Christian Century*, no. 97 (1980): 1094–99. See also W. Brueggemann, "Covenant as Human Vocation: Discussion of the Relation of Bible and Pastoral Care," in *Bonded with the Immortal*, ed. J. M Ford (Wilmington, DE: Michael Glazier, 1987).

10. Nontombi Naomi Tutu, "The Prophetic Future of Christianity," *Oneing* 7, no. 2, *The Future of Christianity* (Fall 2019): 80–81, 82.

11. S. A. Woods and Michael A. West, *The Psychology of Work and Organizations*, 3rd ed. (London: Cemage, 2010).

12. Kelly Hannum et al., eds., *Leading across Differences* (San Francisco: Pfeiffer, 2010), 149.

13. Hannum, *Leading across Differences*, 147–54.

14. Hannum, *Leading across Differences*, 151.

15. Hannum, *Leading across Differences*, 152.

16. Gula, *Just Ministry: Professional Ethics For Pastoral Ministers*.

17. Moses Pava, *Leading with Meaning: Using Covenantal Leadership to Build a Better Organization* (New York: Palgrave MacMillan, 2003), 6–7ff.

18. Cam Caldwell and Zuhair Hasan, "The Covenantal Leader: Honoring the Implicit Relationship with Employees," https://www.researchgate.net/publication/305474361_Insights_from_Covenantal_Leadership.

19. Pava, *Leading with Meaning*.

20. Caldwell and Hasan, "The Covenantal Leader."

21. Brown, *How to Be an Inclusive Leader*.

22. Juana Bordas, *Salsa, and Spirit: Leadership for a Multicultural Age*, 2nd ed. (Oakland, CA: Berrett-Koehler, 2012).

23. June Jordan, *Directed by Desire: The Complete Poems of June Jordan* (Port Townsend, WA: Copper Canyon Press, 2005, 2017).

24. Brenda J. Allen, *Difference Matters: Communicating Social Identity* (Long Grove, IL: Waveland Press, 2011), 185–88.

CHAPTER 5: CREATING A NEW STORY

1. Kathleen Cahalan, *Introducing the Practice of Ministry* (Collegeville, MN: Liturgical Press), 48.

2. Cahalan, *Introducing the Practice of Ministry*, 39.

3. United States Conference of Catholic Bishops, *Co-workers in the Vineyard of the Lord: A Resource for Guiding the Development of Lay Ecclesial Ministry* (2005), 61.

4. Michael P. Leiter and Christina Maslach, "Six Areas of Worklife: A Model of the Organization of the Context of Burnout," *Journal of Health and Human Services Administration* 21, no. 4 (February 1999): 472–89.

5. Joseph E. Champoux, *Organizational Behavior: Integrating Individuals, Groups, and Organizations*, 4th ed. (New York: Routledge, 2010), 11; Bernard M. Bass and Ralph M. Stogdill, *Bass Stogdill's Handbook of Leadership: Theory, Research, and Managerial Application*, 3rd ed. (New York: Free Press, 1990), 3.

6. Ronald Beebe, "Predicting Burnout, Conflict Management Style, and Turnover among Clergy," *Journal of Career Assessment* 15, no. 2 (2007): 257–75.

7. Quentin R. Skrabec Jr., *St. Benedict's Rule for Business Success* (West Lafayette, IN: Purdue University Press, 2003), 15.

Notes

8. John Paul II, Post-synodal Apostolic Exhortation, *Ecclesia in Asia* (November 6, 1999), 24. https://www.vatican.va/content/john-paul-ii/en/apost_exhortations/documents/hf_jp-ii_exh_06111999_ecclesia-in-asia.html.

9. Catherine Mowry LaCugna, *God for Us: The Trinity and Christian Life* (San Francisco: Harper, 1991), 382.

10. Terrence G. Kardong, OSB, *Benedict's Rule: A Translation and a Commentary* (Collegeville, MN: Liturgical Press, 1996), 107.

11. Canon 204, §1, in *Code of Canon Law: Latin-English Edition* (Washington, DC: Canon Law Society of America, 1999).

12. *Co-workers*, 61.

13. *Co-workers*, 61.

14. *Co-workers*, 63.

15. Quintus Septimius Florens Tertullian, *Tertullian: Apology; De Spectaculis*, trans. T. R. Glover, Minucius Felix, Gerald Rendall, and W. C. A. Kerr (London: W. Heinemann, 1953), ch. 39.

16. *Co-workers*, 21.

17. John Paul II, *Laborem Exercens* (1981), 9. https://www.vatican.va/content/john-paul-ii/en/encyclicals/documents/hf_jp-ii_enc_14091981_laborem-exercens.html.

18. Leiter and Maslach, "Six Areas of Worklife," 472–89.

19. Matt Bloom, *Flourishing in Ministry: How to Cultivate Clergy Wellbeing* (Lanham, MD: Rowan & Litchfield, 2019), 25.

20. Teresa Coda, "As Lay Ministries Flourish, Overworked Ministers Struggle with Burnout," *U.S. Catholic* 84, no. 11 (2019): 32–37.

21. *Frequently Requested Church Statistics* (Washington, DC: Center for Applied Research in the Apostolate, 2019), https://www.usccb.org/upload/lem-summit-2015-cara-presentation.pdf.

22. Christina Maslach, *Burnout: The Cost of Caring* (Los Altos, CA: Malor Books, 2015), 2.

23. Philip Zimbardo, *Psychology and Life* (Boston: Addison-Wesley, 1985), 275.

24. Tiiu Kamdron, "Work Motivation: Relationships with Job Satisfaction, Locus of Control and Motivation Orientation," *International Journal of Liberal Arts and Social Science* 3, no. 6 (August 2015): 125–46.

25. Gert Hofstede, Gert Jan Hofstede, and Michael Minkov, *Cultures and Organizations: Software of the Mind* (New York: McGraw Hill, 2010), 92.

26. *Co-workers*, 8.

27. Paul E. Spector, "Perceived Control by Employees: A Meta-analysis of Studies Concerning Autonomy and Participation at Work," *Human Relations* 39, no. 11 (1986): 1005–16.

28. Steve Bradley, Jim Taylor, and Ngoc Anh, "Job Autonomy and Job Satisfaction: New Evidence," *Research Gate*, 2003, https://www.researchgate.net/publication/5161837_Job_autonomy_and_job_satisgaction_new_evidence.

29. Daniel Wheatley, "Autonomy in Paid Work and Employee Subjective Well-being," *Work and Occupations* 44, no. 3 (2017): 296–328.

30. Albert Bandura, "Self-Efficacy Mechanism in Human Agency," *American Psychologist* 37, no. 2 (1982): 122–47.

31. K. K. Ganguly, "Life of M. K. Gandhi: A Message to Youth of Modern India," *India Journal of Medical Research* (January 2019): 149 (Suppl 1): S 145–S 151.

32. Albert Bandura, *Self-Efficacy in Changing Societies* (Cambridge: Cambridge University Press, 1997), 11.

33. *Mad Men*, season 4, episode 7, "The Suitcase," directed by Jennifer Getzinger, written by Matthew Weiner, Brett Johnson, and Erin Levy, aired September 5, 2010, on AMC.

34. Robert W. Kolodinsky, Robert A. Giacalone, and Carole L. Jurkiewicz, "Workplace Values and Outcomes: Exploring Personal, Organizational, and Interactive Workplace Spirituality," *Journal of Business Ethics* 81, no. 2 (2008): 465–80.

35. *Co-workers*, 12.

36. Constitution on the Sacred Liturgy, *Sacrosanctum Concilium* 14: "Mother Church earnestly desires that all the faithful should be led to that fully conscious, and active participation in liturgical celebrations which is demanded by the very nature of the liturgy. Such participation by the Christian people as 'a chosen race, a royal priesthood, a holy nation, a redeemed people' (1 Pet. 2:9; cf. 2:4–5) is their right and duty by reason of their baptism."

37. Maslach, *Banishing Burnout*, 2–3.

38. Hosffman Ospino, *Hispanic Ministry in Catholic Parishes: A Summary Report of Findings from the National Study of Catholic Parishes with Hispanic Ministry* (Chestnut Hill, MA: Boston College, 2014), https://drive.google.com/file/d/1zikFiGJXroEASgQf8QyHL4yTOcDcwHJM/view.

39. Ospino, *Hispanic Ministry*, 19.

Notes

40. Brett C. Hoover, *The Shared Parish: Latinos, Anglos, and the Future of U.S. Catholicism* (New York: New York University Press, 2014), 108.

41. Mark M. Gray, Mary L. Gautier, and Melissa A. Cidade, *The Changing Face of U.S. Catholic Parishes* (Washington, DC: CARA, 2011), 43–47.

42. Michael P. Leiter, Christina Maslach, and Susan E. Jackson, *Maslach Burnout Toolkit for Human Services Individual Report* (Menlo Park, CA: Mind Garden, 2018), 8.

43. *Co-workers*, 8.

44. Richard M. Gula, *Just Ministry: Professional Ethics for Pastoral Ministers* (Mahwah, NJ: Paulist Press, 2010), 45.

45. Maslach, *Burnout*, 2.

46. Wilke Au and Noreen Cannon, *Urgings of the Heart: A Spirituality of Integration* (Mahwah, NJ: Paulist Press, 1995), 96.

47. Thomas W. Frazier, *Dysfunction in Ministry* (Garden Grove, CA, 2013), 141.

48. Frazier, *Dysfunction in Ministry*, 141.

49. Frazier, *Dysfunction in Ministry*, 142.

50. Bloom, *Flourishing Ministry*, 22–26.

51. Robert J. Wicks, *Bounce: Living the Resilient Life* (New York: Oxford University Press, 2010), 53.

52. Au and Cannon, *Urgings of the Heart*, 111.

53. *Co-workers*, 20.

54. Edward P. Hahnenberg, *Ministries: A Relational Approach* (New York: Crossroad, 2003), 121.

55. Richard Robert Osmer, *Practical Theology: An Introduction* (Grand Rapids, MI: Eerdmans, 2008), 178.

56. Osmer, *Practical Theology*, 178.

57. Osmer, *Practical Theology*, 194.

58. *Co-workers*, 21.

59. Hahnenberg, *Ministries*, 92.

60. Mary Jo Bane, "Voice and Loyalty in the Church: The People of God, Politics and Management," in *Common Calling: The Laity and Governance of the Catholic Church*, ed. Stephen J. Pope (Washington, DC: Georgetown University Press, 2004), 191–92.

61. Bane, "Voice and Loyalty in the Church," 191–92.

62. Lexico.com, s.v. "Fairness," accessed December 16, 2019.

63. Bruce Weinstein, *The Good Ones: Ten Crucial Qualities of High-Character Employees* (Novato, CA: New World Library, 2015), 114.

64. William P. Macaux, "Engagement, Fairness, and Care," Generativity LLC, 2015, https://generativityllc.com/blog/engagement-fairness-and-care.

65. Maslach, *Burnout*, 5.

66. Barbara Reid, OP, "The Gospel according to Matthew," in *New Collegeville Bible Commentary: New Testament*, ed. Daniel Durken (Collegeville, MN: Liturgical Press, 2009), 63.

67. Reid, "The Gospel according to Matthew," 63.

68. Katherine M. Hayes, "The Book of Proverbs," in *New Collegeville Bible Commentary: Old Testament*, ed. Daniel Durken (Collegeville, MN: Liturgical Press, 2015), 1103.

69. Aquinata Boöckmann, *Perspectives on the Rule of St. Benedict* (Collegeville, MN: Liturgical Press, 2005), 38.

70. Saint Benedict, *RB80: The Rule of Saint Benedict in Latin and English with Notes*, ed. by Timothy Fry, OSB (Collegeville, MN: Liturgical Press, 1981), 177.

71. Birgit Kleymann and Hedley Malloch, *The Rule of Saint Benedict and Corporate Management: Employing the Whole Person* (Lille, France: Catholic University of Lille, 2010), https://www.researchgate.net/publication/242336203_The_Rule_of_Saint_Benedict_and_Corporate_Management_Employing_the_Whole_Person.

72. Jill Schiefelbein, *Dynamic Communication: 27 Strategies to Grow, Lead, and Manage Your Business* (Irvine, CA: Entrepreneur Press, 2017). See also "6 Ways to Tell If Your Workplace Is Fair," *Fast Company*, Sept. 4, 2014, https://www.Fastcompany.com/3035177/6-ways-to-tell-if-your-workplace-is-fair.

73. *Evangelii Gaudium* 150.

74. *Evangelii Gaudium* 3–75.

75. CARA, *Lay Ecclesial Ministers in the United States*, 11.

76. *Brockmeyer v. Dun & Bradstreet* (Justia US Law, 1983), chap 2. Under English common law, an employment contract for an indefinite period was presumed to extend for one year unless there was reasonable cause to discharge. The English rule had evolved from the Statute of Labourers, which provided that "no master can put away his servant." Early American courts followed this approach. In the late nineteenth century, apparently influenced by the laissez-faire climate of the Industrial Revolution, the American courts then rejected the English rule and developed their own common-law rule, the *567 employment at-will doctrine. The doctrine recognized that where an employment was for

Notes

an indefinite term, an employer may discharge an employee "for good cause, for no cause, or even for cause morally wrong, without being thereby guilty of legal wrong."

77. Pope Leo XIII, *Rerum Novarum* (1891) 37.
78. *Co-workers*, 64.
79. *Co-workers*, 64.
80. "Research Review: Lay Ecclesial Ministers in the United States," 21.
81. *The Changing Face of U.S. Catholic Parishes*, 1–77.
82. "What Is Certification?" (Alliance for Certification of Lay Ecclesial Ministers), www.lemcertification.org/.
83. Rosie Ward and Jon Robison, *How to Build a Thriving Culture at Work* (Kalamazoo, MI: IHAC, 2015), 165.
84. Pope John Paul II, *Laborem Exercens* 19.
85. "Research Review: Lay Ecclesial Ministers in the United States," 22.
86. "How Catholic Churches Spend Money" (March 11, 2018), https://tomshakely.com/2018/how-catholic-Churches-spend-money/.
87. Brian Fraga, "In Response to Abuse Crisis, More Catholics Are Withholding Financial Gifts from the Church," *America* 221 (2019), https://www.americamagazine.org/politics-society/2019/09/17/response-abuse-crisis-more-catholics-are-withholding-financial-gifts.
88. Joseph Cardinal Tobin, "Reflection of His Eminence Joseph Cardinal Tobin," Archbishop of Newark: Evening of Witness and Praise, Convocation of Catholic Leaders (Orlando, FL, Hyatt Regency, 2017), 1.
89. *Stewardship, A Disciple's Response: A Pastoral Letter on Stewardship* (Washington, DC: USCCB Publishing, 2002), 43.
90. *Co-workers*, 15.

CHAPTER 6: THE WAY FORWARD

1. Howard Gardner and Lee S. Shulman, "Daedalus," *On Professions & Professionals* 134, no. 3 (Summer 2005): 13–18.

APPENDIX C: LEARNING FROM OUR STORIES

1. Lee S. Schulman, "Signature Pedagogies in the Professions," *Daedalus* 134, no. 3 (2005): 52–59.
2. Priya Parker, *The Art of Gathering: How We Meet and Why It Matters* (New York: Riverhead Books, 2020), 1–34.

BIBLIOGRAPHY

Adichie, Chimanda Ngozi. "The Danger of a Single Story." TED Talks, August 7, 2016. https://www.ted.com/talks/chimamanda_ngozi_adichie_the_danger_of_a_single_story.

Allen, Brenda J. *Differences Matters: Communicating Social Identity*. Long Grove, IL: Waveland Press, 2011.

Au, Wilkie, and Noreen Cannon. *Urgings of the Heart: A Spirituality of Integration*. Mahwah, NJ: Paulist Press, 1995.

Bandura, Albert. "Self-Efficacy Mechanism in Human Agency." *American Psychologist,* 1982.

———. *Self-Efficacy in Changing Societies*. Cambridge: Cambridge University Press, 1997.

Bane, Mary Jo. "Voice and Loyalty in the Church: The People of God, Politics and Management." In *Common Calling: The Laity and Governance of the Catholic Church*. Edited by Stephen J. Pope, 191–92. Washington, DC: Georgetown University Press, 2004.

Bass, Bernard M., and Ralph M. Stogdill. *Bass Stogdill's Handbook of Leadership: Theory, Research, and Managerial Application*. 3rd ed. New York: Free Press, 1990.

Benedict. *RB80: The Rule of St. Benedict in Latin and English with Notes*. Edited by Timothy Fry, OSB. Collegeville, MN: Liturgical Press, 1981.

Block, Peter. *Community: The Structure of Belonging*. San Francisco: Berrett-Koehler, 2008.

Bloom, Matt. *Flourishing in Ministry: How to Cultivate Clergy Wellbeing*. New York: Rowman & Littlefield, 2019.

Böckmann, Aquinata. *Perspectives of the Rule of St. Benedict*. Collegeville, MN: Liturgical Press, 2005.

Bradley, Steve, Jim Taylor, and Ngoc Anh. "Job Autonomy and Job Satisfaction: New Evidence." Research Gate, 2003.

Brockmeyer v. Dun Bradstreet. Justia US Law, 1983.

Brooks, David. *The Second Mountain: The Quest for a Moral Life*. New York: Random House, 2020.

Brown, Jennifer. *How to Be an Inclusive Leader: Your Role in Creating Cultures of Belonging Where Everyone Can Thrive*. Oakland, CA: Barrett-Koehler Publisher, 2019.

Brueggemann, Walter. "Covenant as a Subversive Paradigm" *The Christian Century*, 1980.

———. "Covenant as Human Vocation: Discussion of the Relation of Bible and Pastoral Care." In *Bonded with the Immortal*, edited by J. M. Ford. Wilmington, DE: Michael Glazier, 1987.

Buechner, Frederick. *Wishful Thinking: A Seeker's ABC*. New York: HarperOne, 1993.

Bush, Michael. *Leaders: "Your Organization Needs You More Than Ever."* 2022.

Cahalan, Kathleen A. *Introduction to the Practice of Ministry*. Collegeville, MN: Liturgical Press, 2010.

Caldwell, Cam, and Zuhair Hasan. "The Covenantal Leader: Honoring the Implicit Relationship with Employees." *Insights from Covenantal Leadership*. https://www.researchgate.net/publication/305474361.

Champoux, Joseph E. *Organizational Behavior: Integrating Individuals, Groups, and Organizations*. 4th ed. New York: Routledge, 2010.

Chittister, Joan. *The Monastic Heart: 50 Simple Practices for a Contemplative and Fulfilling Life*. New York: Convergent, 2021.

The Church as a Field Hospital: Caring for Our Own; A Position Paper of the National Association for Lay Ministry to Our Bishops and Those Tasked with Carrying Out Their Directives. National Association for Lay Ecclesial Ministry, 2022.

Coda, Teresa. "As Lay Ministries Flourish, Overworked Ministers Struggle with Burnout." *U.S. Catholic* 84, no. 11 (2019): 32–37.

Code of Canon Law: Latin-English Edition. Washington, DC: Canon Law Society of America, 1999.

Co-workers in the Vineyard of the Lord: A Resource for Guiding the Development of Lay Ecclesial Ministry. Washington, DC: United States Conference of Catholic Bishops, 2005.

Bibliography

Deloitte and Victorian Equal Opportunity and Human Rights Commission. "Waiter, Is That Inclusion in My Soup? A New Recipe to Improve Business Performance." https://www2.deloitte.com/content/dam/Deloitte/au/Documents/human-capital/deloitte-au-hc-diversity-inclusion-soup-0513.pdf?bingParse, May 2013.

DeMers, Jason. "Research Says This Is the Secret to Being Happy at Work." NBC Universal, May 22, 2017. https://www.nbcnews.com/better/careers/research-says-secret-being-happy-work-n762926.

Ferdman, B. M., V. Barrera, A. Allen, and V. Vuong. "Inclusive Behavior and the Experience of Inclusion." *What Makes an Organization Inclusive: Measures, HR, Practices and Climate*. Symposium presented at the Annual Meeting of the Academy of Management, Chicago, August 2009.

Fraga, Brian. "In Response to Abuse Crisis, More Catholics Are Withholding Financial Gifts from the Church." *America*, September 19, 2019. https://www.americamagazine.org/politics-society/2019/09/17/response-abuse-crisis-more-catholics-are-withholding-financial-gifts.

Francis, Pope. *Evangelii Gaudium*. Vatican City: Libreria Editrice Vaticana, 2013.

Frazier, Thomas W., PhD. *Dysfunctions in Ministry*. Garden Grove, CA: 2013.

Frequently Requested Church Statistics. Washington, DC: Center for Applied Research in the Apostolate, 2019. https://cara.georgetown.edu/faqs.

Gandhi, Mahatma. *The Collected Works of Mahatma Gandhi*. New Delhi: Publications Division, Ministry of Information and Broadcasting, Govt. of India, 1869–1948.

Gray, Mark M., Mary L. Gautier, and Melissa A. Cidade. *The Changing Face of U.S Catholic Parishes*. Washington, DC: National Association for Lay Ministry, 2011.

Gudykunst, William B. "An Anxiety/Uncertainty Management Theory of Effective Communication." In *Theorizing Intercultural Communication*, ch. 13. Thousand Oaks, CA: Sage Publications, 2005.

Gula, Richard M. *Just Ministry: Professional Ethics for Pastoral Ministers*. Mahwah, NJ: Paulist Press, 2010.

Hahnenberg, Edward P. *Ministries: A Relational Approach*. New York: Crossroad, 2003.

Hall, Edward T. *The Hidden Dimensions*. New York: Anchor Books, 1969.
Hannum, Kelly, Belinda B. McFeeters, and Lize Booysen, eds. *Leading across Differences*. San Francisco: John Wiley & Sons, 2010.
Harvey, Tara. "Intercultural Learning." Online course notes. True North Intercultural, 2020.
Hayes, Katherine M. "The Book of Proverbs." In *New Collegeville Bible Commentary: Old Testament*, edited by Daniel Durken. Collegeville, MN: Liturgical Press, 2015.
Hofstede, Geert, Gert Jan Hofstede, and Michael Minkov. *Cultures and Organizations: Software of the Mind*. New York: McGraw-Hill, 2010.
Hofstede, Gert Jan, Paul B. Pedersen, and Geert Hofstede. *Exploring Culture: Exercises, Stories and Synthetic Cultures*. London: Intercultural Press, 2002.
Hong, Angie. "Women of Color in Ministry Are Not Scarce, Just Unsupported." Bearings Online, February 3, 2022. https://collegevilleinstitute.org/bearings/women-of-color-in-ministry-are-not-scarce-just-unsupported/.
Hoover, Brett C. *The Shared Parish: Latinos, Anglos, and the Future of U.S. Catholicism*. New York: New York University Press, 2014.
Horwitz, C. *The Love That Does Justice: Spiritual Activism in Dialogue with Social Justices*. Edited by M. A. Edwards and S. G. Post, 53–56. Stony Brook, NY: Unlimited Love Press.
Jewell, Marti R., and Mark Mogilka. *"Open Wide the Doors to Christ": A Study of Catholic Social Innovation for Parish Vitality*. Fadica, 2020. https://www.hiltonfoundation.org/wp-content/uploads/2020/08/Open-Wide-the-Doors-to-Christ—A-Study-of-Catholic-Social-Innovation-for-Parish-Vitality-Executive-Summary.pdf.
John Paul II, Pope. *Laborem Exercens*. Vatican City: Libreria Editrice Vaticana, 1981. vatican.va/content/john-paul-ii/en/encyclicals/documents/hf_jp-ii_enc_14091981_laborem-exercens.html.
Jordan, June. *Directed by Desire: The Complete Poems of June Jordan*. Port Townsend, WA: Copper Canyon Press, 2005, 2017.
Kamdron, Tiiu. "Work Motivation: Relationships with Job Satisfaction, Locus of Control and Motivation Orientation." *International Journal of Liberal Arts and Social Science*, 2015.
Kardong, Terrence G., OSB. *Benedict's Rule: A Translation and a Commentary*. Collegeville, MN: The Liturgical Press, 1996.

Bibliography

Kleymann, Birgit, and Hedley Malloch. *The Rule of Saint Benedict and Corporate Management: Employing the Whole Person*. Lille: Catholic University of Lille, 2010. https://www.researchgate.net/publication/242336203_The_Rule_of_Saint_Benedict_and_Corporate_Management_Employing_the_Whole_Person.

Kluckhohn, C., and A. L. Kroeber, eds. *Culture*. New York: Random House, 1952.

Kolodinsky, Robert W., Robert A. Giacalone, and Carole L. Jurkiewicz. "Workplace Values and Outcomes: Exploring Personal, Organizational, and Interactive Workplace Spirituality." *Journal of Business Ethics* 81, no. 2 (2008).

Leiter, Michael P., and Christina Maslach. *Banishing Burnout: Six Strategies for Improving Your Relationship with Work*. San Francisco: Jossey-Bass, 2005.

Leiter, Michael, and Christina Maslach. "Six Areas of Work-Life: A Model of the Organizational Context of Burnout." *Journal of Health and Human Services Administration,* 1999.

Leiter, Michael P., Christina Maslach, and Susan E. Jackson. *Maslach Burnout Toolkit for Human Services Individual Report*. Menlo Park, CA: Mind Garden, Inc., 2018.

Leiter, Michael, Christina Maslach, and Susan Jackson. *Six Areas of Work-life: A Model of the Organization Context of Burnout*. Hoboken, NJ: Jossey-Bass, 2008.

Leo XIII, Pope. *Rerum Novarum*. Vatican City: Libreria Editrice Vaticana, 1891.

Lingenfelter, Sherwood G. *Leading Cross Culturally: Covenant Relationships for Effective Christian Leadership*. Grand Rapids, MI: Baker Academic, 2008.

Livermore, David A. *Cultural Intelligence: Improving Your CQ to Engage Our Multicultural World*. Grand Rapids, MI: Baker Academic, 2009.

Macaux, William P. "Engagement, Fairness, and Care." Generativity LLC, 2015. https://generativityllc.com/blog/engagement-fairness-and-care.

Maslach, Christina. *Burnout: The Cost of Caring*. Cambridge, MA: Malor Books, 2015.

McLaren, Brian. *Finding Our Way Again: The Return of the Ancient Practices*. Nashville: Thomas Nelson, 2008.

Moreau, A. Scott, Evvy Hay Campbell, and Susan Greener. *Effective Intercultural Communication*. Grand Rapids, MI: Baker Academic, 2014.

Newberg, Andrew B., and Mark Robert Waldman. *How God Changes Your Brain: Breakthrough Findings from a Leading Neuroscientist*. New York: Ballentine Books, 2009.

Osmer, Richard Robert. *Practical Theology: An Introduction*. Grand Rapids, MI: William B. Eerdmans, 2008.

Ospino, Hosffman. *Hispanic Ministry in Catholic Parishes: A Summary Report of Findings from the National Study of Catholic Parishes with Hispanic Ministry*. Huntington, IN: Our Sunday Visitor, 2015.

Palmer, Parker. "Leading from Within." *Let Your Life Speak: Listening for the Voice of Vocation*. Hoboken, NJ: John Wiley, 2000.

Parker, Priya. *Art of Gathering: How We Meet and Why It Matters*. New York: Riverhead Books, 2020.

Pava, Moses. *Leading with Meaning: Using Covenantal Leadership to Build a Better Organization*. New York: Palgrave MacMillan, 2003.

Pfeffer, Jeffrey. *Dying for a Paycheck: How Modern Management Harms Employee Health and Company Performance—and What We Can Do About It*. New York: Harper-Collins, 2018.

Reid, Barbara, OP. "The Gospel According to Matthew." In *New Collegeville Bible Commentary: New Testament*, edited by Daniel Durken. Collegeville, MN: Liturgical Press, 2009.

"Research Review: Lay Ecclesial Ministers in the United States." Washington, DC: Center for Applied Research in the Apostolate (CARA), Georgetown University, 2015.

Saigoneer. "Study: Divorce Is Up Significantly in Vietnam." https://saigoneer.com/vietnam-news/2592-study-divorce-is-up-significantly-in-vietnam.

Schiefelbein, Jill. *Dynamic Communication: 27 Strategies to Grow, Lead, and Manage Your Business*. Irvine, CA: Entrepreneur Press, 2017.

Schein, Edgar. *Organizational Culture and Leadership*. San Francisco: Jossey-Bass, 2004.

Shakely, Tom. "How Catholic Churches Spend Money." March 11, 2018. https://tomshakely.com/2018/how-catholic-churches-spend-money/.

Skrabec, Quentin R., Jr. *St. Benedict's Rule for Business Success*. West Lafayette, IN: Purdue University Press, 2003.

Bibliography

Spector, Paul E. "Perceived Control by Employees: A Meta-Analysis of Studies Concerning Autonomy and Participation at Work." *Human Relations,* 1986.

Spoon, Bryan. *Neuroscience and the Fruit of the Spirit.* Glendale: WI: Talk Publishing, 2020.

Steidle, Gretchen K. *Leading from Within: Conscious Social Change and Mindfulness for Social Innovation.* Cambridge, MA: MIT Press, 2018.

Stewardship, A Disciple's Response: A Pastoral Letter on Stewardship. Washington, DC: USCCB Publishing, 2002.

Tertullian, Quintus Septimius Florens. *Tertullian: Apology; De Spectaculis.* Translated by T. R. Glover, Minucius Felix, Gerald Rendall, and W. C. A. Kerr. London: W. Heinemann, 1953.

"Time Management." *Cambridge Dictionary.* Cambridge: Cambridge University Press, 2020. https://dictionary.cambridge.org/us/dictionary/english/time-management.

Tobin, Joseph Cardinal. *Reflection of His Eminence Joseph Cardinal Tobin, Archbishop of Newark: Evening of Witness and Praise, Convocation of Catholic Leaders.* Orlando, FL, Hyatt Regency, 2017.

"Toward Canonical Consideration of the Authorization of Lay Ecclesial Ministers for Ministry." Saint John's School of Theology and Seminary, 2015. https://www.csbsju.edu/lemsymposium.

Tutu, Nontombi Naomi. "The Prophetic Future of Christianity." *Oneing* 7, no. 2, *The Future of Christianity,* Fall 2019.

2007 National Symposium on Lay Ecclesial Ministry. Saint John's School of Theology and Seminary, 2007. https://www.csbsju.edu/sot/sem/lifelong-learning/lay-ecclesial-ministry/2007-national-symposium-on-lay-ecclesial-ministry.

United States Conference of Catholic Bishops. *U.S. National Synthesis 2021–2023 Synod.* https://www.usccb.org/resources/us-national-synthesis-2021-2023-synod.

U.S. Census Bureau. "Currently Divorced People as a Percent of People Who Have Ever Been Married." USAFacts. https://usafacts.org/data/topics/people-society/population-and-demographics/population-data/net-divorce-rate-currently-divorced-as-of-ever-married.

———. "Year of Birth by Current Marital Status, Whether First Marriage Ended, Number of Times, Race, and Sex for Person Born between 1900 and 1954." June 1971. https://www2.census.gov/

programs-surveys/demo/tables/marriage-and-divorce/1971/p20-239-1972-t1.pdf.

Ward, Rosie, and Jon Robison. *How to Build a Thriving Culture at Work*. Kalamazoo, MI: IHAC, 2015.

Watanabe, Teresa. "A Divine View of Van Gogh." *Los Angeles Times*, January 23, 1999. https://www.latimes.com/archives/la-xpm-1999-jan-23-me-835-story.html.

Weiner, Matthew, Brett Johnson, and Erin Levy. "The Suitcase." *Mad Men*. Season 4, episode 7. Directed by Jennifer Getzinger. Aired September 5, 2010, on AMC.

Weinstein, Bruce. *The Good Ones: Ten Crucial Qualities of High-Character Employees*. Novato, CA: New World Library, 2015.

West, M. S., J. Lyubovnikova, R. Eckert, and J. L. Denis. "Collective Leadership for Cultures of High-Quality Healthcare." *Journal of Organizational Effectiveness: People and Performance* 1, no. 3 (2014).

Wheatley, Daniel. "Autonomy in Paid Work and Employee Subjective Well-Being." *Work and Occupations* (2017).

Wicks, Robert J. *Bounce: Living the Resilient Life*. New York: Oxford University Press, 2010.

Woods, S. A., and Michael A. West. *The Psychology of Work and Organizations*. 3rd ed. London: Cemage, 2010.

Yeager, Katherine A., and Susan Bauer-Wu. "Cultural Humility: Essential Foundation for Clinical Researchers." NIH: National Library of Medicine, 2013. https://pubmed.ncbi.nlm.nih.gov/23938129/.

Zannoni, Arthur E. "The Biblical Covenant: Bonding with God." Presentation notes shared by the author.

Zimbardo, Philip. *Psychology and Life*. Boston: Addison-Wesley, 1985.

INDEX

abuse scandal, 3
action, 170
Adichie, Chimamanda Ngozi, 43–44
Allen, Brenda, 100
Apostolic Exhortation to the Church in Asia, 111
Areas of Work-Life Survey (AWS), 32, 33–34
Art of Gathering, The, 168
assessment tool, 8–9
assimilation, 63
assumptions, 90–91
attitudes, 72–73
at-will employment, 140–41
autonomy, 121
"Average Household Weekly Offertory by Parish Ethnic Composition," 128

balance, 131
Banishing Burnout, 125–26
baptismal call, 129–30
Bazan, Jessie, 1
Benedictine tradition, 109, 110, 137–39
biases, 90–91
Bivens, Kristi, 5

Block, Peter, 40
Bloom, Matt, 117, 131
body of Christ, 109
Bordas, Juana, 93
Brooks, David, 104, 105
Brown, Jennifer, 65, 84, 93
Brueggemann, Walter, 86
Buechner, Frederick, 6, 81
burnout, 23, 32–33, 125–26, 130, 134
Burnout Toolkit for Human Services Individual Report, 128
Bush, Michael, 29

Cahalan, Kathleen, 104, 105, 107
Canon Law Society of America (CLSA), 26
Center for Applied Research in the Apostolate (CARA), 26, 140
Center of Creative Leadership, 55, 88
chaplaincy, 109
charism, 129
charismatic renewal, 129–30
Chittister, Joan, 73–74
Choinier, Robert, 9
Church, the, 112–16, 125

Church Workplace Standards: A Self-Audit, 26
CliftonStrengths Indicator, 70
clinical pastoral education (CPE), 7
communication, 100, 170–71
communion ecclesiology, 132–33
community, 34, 109–11, 113, 155
Community: The Structure of Belonging, 40
conflict, 62–64
continuing education, 145
control, 35, 117–22, 156
conversation, 171–72
covenant, 41: and agency, 82; and contract, 88–89, 140; culture, 41, 81; and employment, 139–40; and freedom, 89; and God, 3, 81, 85–87, 99; and identity, 80–81; and lay ecclesial ministers, 3, 140; and leadership, 91–94; and love, 89; ministry, 83–84, 94–95, 147; principles, 96–98; relationships, 81–82; responsibility, 84–85, 92–93; statement, 83–84, 94–96, 158–59; and trust, 87–91; and vocation, 88; and workload, 128
Covenant-Based Reflection Guide for Ministerial Workplaces, 161–65
Co-workers in the Vineyard of the Lord, 25, 26, 27–28, 103, 119, 124, 129, 141, 142
culture: achievement/nurturance, 53, 55; bridge-building, 72–75; and control, 119; covenant, 41, 81; cultural dimensions theory, 50; cultural humility, 44, 58, 82; defined, 44; differences, 44–45, 55–56, 72–75, 146; direct/indirect communication orientation, 53–54, 55; generational cohort, 69–70; iceberg model, 46–49; identity, 58, 67–70, 146; individualism/collectivism, 50, 54; individual personality, 48; and intercultural learning, 24; lens, 45; long-term/short-term orientation, 52, 54; national, 46; organizational, 24; power distance, 51, 54; triggers, 73–74; uncertainty avoidance, 51, 54; unspoken rules, 47; values, 47–48, 60, 72
curiosity, 90

David, 3, 4
depersonalization, 18, 32
development, organizational, 17
diaconate, 10–11
Diane, 72
differences: bridging, 72–75; culture, 44–45, 55–56, 72–75, 146; fault lines, 64–66; and identities, 57, 67, 146; identity conflict, 62–64; inclusion, 65–66; intentionality, 90; and spillover, 61–62; strengths, 70–71; team, 67–68; values, 63; and the workplace, 44, 80
differential treatment, 63
dignity, 125

Index

discernment, 2
divorce, 64
dominant/non-dominant groups, 87–88
Dying for a Paycheck, 29
dysfunction, 131

Emmaus Institute for Ministry Formation, 6
emotional exhaustion, 32
employment, 139–40
Engagement, Fairness and Care, 134
Eucharist, 124–25
Evangelii Gaudium, 139

fairness, 36, 133–38, 154–55
fair outcomes, 134, 135
fair processes, 134–35
Ferdman, B. M., 66
field hospital, 28, 29
figuring it out, 13
finances. *See* money
financial well-being, 34, 39
Finding Our Way Again, 31
Flourishing in Ministry, 117, 131
Floyd, George, 61
Francis, Pope, 29, 118, 139
Frazier, Thomas W., 131
fundraising, 19, 21–22

Gandhi, Mahatma, 121
gender, 62
giftedness, 129
God: blessings, 4; community, 77–78, 111; and covenant, 3, 81, 85–87, 99; trust, 89; vineyard, 31
Good Ones, The, 133–34

Great Resignation, The, 61
Gula, Richard, 84, 88–89

Hannum, Kelly, 88
Hayes, Katherine M., 137
health, 29–30, 146
healthcare, 117–18, 141–42
Healthy Ministerial Workplace Covenant Assessment, 151
healthy spiritual life, 130–31
hierarchy, 24, 78, 81, 147
Hispanics, 127–28
Hofstede, Geert, 50
Holy Spirit, 75, 125, 129
Hong, Angie, 30
Hoover, Bret, 128
Horwitz, Claudia, 41
How to Be an Inclusive Leader, 84
hyperindividualism, 105
hypocrisy, 116

identities: conflict, 62–64; core, 59; covenant, 80–81; cultural, 58, 60, 66, 68, 146; and differences, 57, 67, 146; elements, 56–57; generational, 69–70; Mexico, 68; personal, 66–67; self-awareness, 57; social, 59, 66; U.S., 68
identity mapping, 58–59
inclusion, 30, 147
India, 21
individual consciousness, 41
inefficiency, 33
insults or humiliating acts, 63
Intercultural Development Inventory (IDI), 24, 61

In the Name of the Church: Vocation and Authorization of Lay Ecclesial Ministry, 27
Introducing the Practice of Ministry, 104

Jesus Christ, 31, 56, 81, 106, 116, 119, 125
Jewell, Marti, 61
job satisfaction, 110
John Paul II, St., 111, 142
Johnston, Timothy, 18
Jordan, 14–15
Jordan, June, 99, 166–67

Kardong, Terrence G., 111
Kaster, Jeff, 26
Klawitter, Bridget, 11
Klimoski, Victor, 58, 75
knowledge base, 167–68
koinonia, 113
Korth, Mrs., 8–9

LaCugna, Catherine Mowry, 111
lament, 31
Law, Dorice, 7
lay ecclesial ministers (LEMs), 26–27, 30
lay ministers: and abuse scandal, 3; CARA survey, 26–27; control, 117; and covenant, 3, 140; reward, 124–25; Saint John's symposia, 26–27; standards, 25–26; stories, 2–3, 146; and values, 113–14; and vocation, 7, 23, 103, 106–8
Lay Ministry Summit, 27
Leaders: Your Organization Needs You More Than Ever, 29

leadership: and covenant, 91–94; divine spark, 28; education, 142–43; employment, 139–44; and hierarchy, 78; mapping your network, 76–79; Pava, 91–92; relationships, 78–79; responsibilities, 92–93; servant, 132; task competence, 132; transactional, 132; transformational, 132, 134; and the Trinity, 77–78; and trust, 83; values, 10–11
Leading across Differences, 55
Leading Cross-Culturally, 83
Leading from Within, 84
Leading with Meaning, 91
Lechtenberg, Kyle, 14
lectio, 158
Leiter, Michael, 125
Leo XIII, Pope, 141
Lingenfelter, Sherwood G., 83
liturgy, 15
locus of control, 118–19, 122
love, 89, 114–15

Macaux, William P., 134
Macedo, Yaret, 16
Mad Men, 123
Maslach, Christina, 32, 81, 125, 130
Maslach Burnout Inventory (MBI), 32–33, 128
Matthew, Fr., 72
McLaren, Brian, 31
minimization, 24
Mogilka, Mark, 61
money, 19–20, 21–22, 34, 126, 141–43, 154
Morgan, 7–9, 110

Index

motivation, 121
music, 15, 21–22, 141

narratives. *See* stories
National Association for Lay Ministry (NALM), 27
National Association of Church Personnel Administrators (NACPA), 26
National Certification Standards for Lay Ecclesial Ministers, 26
nonmonetary compensation, 126
norms, 169–70

"Open Wide the Doors to Christ: A Study of Catholic Social Innovation for Parish Vitality," 61
organization, 120
Osmer, Richard R., 132
Ospino, Hosffman, 127
overextension, 33

Palmer, Parker, 31
Parker, Priya, 168
pastoral planning, 10
Paul, Apostle, 109–10, 113
Pava, Moses, 91–93
personal accomplishment, 32–33
Pfeffer, Jeffery, 29–30
possibilities, 41
prayer, 101, 170
preaching, 8
prioritization, 13
prodigal son, 136
professional development, 167–68
Proverbs, 137
purpose, 168–69

Reece, 14
Reid, Barbara, 136–37
relationship, 78–79, 81–82, 114–15, 132–33
repatterning, 24
Rerum Novarum, 141
resignations, 17
reward, 36, 122–26, 156–57
Rite of Christian Initiation of Adults (RCIA), 48
routine, 120
rules of engagement, 169
Rule of St. Benedict. *See* Benedictine tradition

sacrifice, 3–4
Saint John's Abbey Guesthouse, 2
Saint John's School of Theology and Seminary, 26–27, 108–9
salaries, 21
Schiefelbein, Jill, 138
Scriptures, 85, 136, 138–39
Second Mountain, The, 104
self-assessment tools, 34–40, 152–57
Shared Parish, The, 128
Shulman, Lee, 145, 167
siloes, 57, 76
simple contact, 63
single life, 5
sourpusses, 28–29
spillover, 61–62
spirituality, organizational, 123–24
spiritual practices, 74–75
Spoon, Bryan, 74–75
Starry Night, 29
statement of workplace covenant, 159

199

Steidle, Gretchen Ki, 84
Stewardship: A Disciple's Response, 140, 144
stories, 2–3, 43–44, 146, 147, 173–74
structure, organizational, 81, 100, 110, 143
Sutton, Barbara, 48–49, 63–64, 67, 70–71, 75
synodal synthesis, 62

thriving, 28
time management, 120
Tobin, Joseph, 143
"Toward Canonical Consideration of the Authorization of Lay Ecclesial Ministers for Ministry," 26
triggers, 62–65, 73–74
Trinity, 77–78, 111
trust, 83, 87–91
truth, 99–100
Tutu, Nontombi Naomi, 86

U.S. Conference of Catholic Bishops (USCCB), 25

values, 38, 112–16, 152–53
van Gogh, Vincent, 29
vicar general, 10–11
vineyard, 23, 28, 31, 110–11
visio divina, 3

vision, 100
vocation: assessment tool, 152; AWS survey, 34, 40; and covenant, 88; definition, 6, 103, 104; how I live, 104–5, 107; "I am" statements, 106–7; lay ministers, 7, 23, 103, 106–8; and single life, 5, 103, 104; what I do, 105, 107; who I am, 105–6, 107

Wahl, James, 20
"We Are the Ones We Have Been Waiting For," 166. *See also* Jordan, June
Weinstein, Bruce, 133–34
West, Michael, 81, 86
White, C. Vanessa, 147–50
Woods, S. A, 86
work culture, 17, 44
workers in the vineyard, 136–37
"Working in the Vineyard: A Statement on Employment Practices for Lay Ecclesial Ministers," 27–28
workload, 18, 29, 37, 127–33, 153
worship, 124

Zannoni, Arthur, 85, 86
Zimbardo, Philip, 118